TF Design
Modern Designs in Resin

tf.design

tf

Mushroom Lamp

Handcraft meets high technology. Made in Berlin.
Photography by Mark Borthwick.

MYKITA

KINFOLK

MAGAZINE
—

EDITOR IN CHIEF	John Clifford Burns
EDITOR	Harriet Fitch Little
ART DIRECTOR	Christian Møller Andersen
DESIGN DIRECTOR	Alex Hunting
COPY EDITOR	Rachel Holzman
FACT CHECKER	Gabriele Dellisanti

STUDIO
—

ADVERTISING, SALES & DISTRIBUTION DIRECTOR	Edward Mannering
STUDIO & PROJECT MANAGER	Susanne Buch Petersen
DESIGNER & ART DIRECTOR	Staffan Sundström
DIGITAL MANAGER	Cecilie Jegsen

—

CROSSWORD	Mark Halpin
PUBLICATION DESIGN	Alex Hunting Studio
COVER PHOTOGRAPHS	Zhonglin
	Michael Oliver Love

WORDS
—

Precious Adesina
Allyssia Alleyne
Alex Anderson
Rima Sabina Aouf
Lavender Au
Zoë Blade
Katie Calautti
Stephanie d'Arc Taylor
Gabriele Dellisanti
Daphnée Denis
Aindrea Emelife
Tom Faber
Bella Gladman
Harry Harris
Robert Ito
Ana Kinsella
Rebecca Liu
Stevie MacKenzie-Smith
Kyla Marshell
Hettie O'Brien
John Ovans
Sala Elise Patterson
Debika Ray
Asher Ross
Baya Simons
Sharine Taylor
George Upton
Anna Winston
Ava Wong Davies

STYLING, SET DESIGN, HAIR & MAKEUP
—

Gemma Bedini
Rahnell Branton
Michelle-Lee Collins
Caitlin Doherty
Christian Feltham
Evan Feng
Alexiane Guyon
Nick Holiday
Gao Jian
Louw Kotze
Lando
Cameron Lee
Fiona Li
Weic Lin
Hu Yiyin
Chen Yu

ARTWORK & PHOTOGRAPHY
—

Paul Atwood
Michael Avedon
Ted Belton
James Bennett
Martina Bjorn
Luc Braquet
Amanda Charchian
Valerie Chiang
Paula Codoner
Oye Diran
Tom Hartford
Evelyn Hofer
Cecilie Jegsen
Risto Kamunen
Charlotte Lapalus
Romain Laprade
German Lorca
Michael Oliver Love
E.E. McCollum
Emman Montalvan
Katya Mukhina
Juan Pantoja
Oumayma B. Tanfous
The Diigitals
Aaron Tilley
Emma Trim
Jumbo Tsui
George Underwood
Alex Wolfe
Zhonglin

PUBLISHER
—

Chul-Joon Park

The views expressed in *Kinfolk* magazine are those of the respective contributors and are not necessarily shared by the company or its staff. *Kinfolk* (ISSN 2596-6154) is published quarterly by Ouur ApS, Amagertorv 14, 1, 1160 Copenhagen, Denmark. Printed by Park Communications Ltd in London, United Kingdom. Color reproduction by Park Communications Ltd in London, United Kingdom. All rights reserved. No part of this publication may be reproduced, distributed or transmitted in any form or by any means, including photocopying or other electronic or mechanical methods, without prior written permission of the editor in chief, except in the case of brief quotations embodied in critical reviews and certain other noncommercial uses permitted by copyright law. The US annual subscription price is $87 USD. Airfreight and mailing in the USA by WN Shipping USA, 156-15, 146th Avenue, 2nd Floor, Jamaica, NY 11434, USA. Application to mail at periodicals postage prices is pending at Jamaica NY 11431. US Postmaster: Send address changes to *Kinfolk*, WN Shipping USA, 156-15, 146th Avenue, 2nd Floor, Jamaica, NY 11434, USA. Subscription records are maintained at Ouur ApS, Amagertorv 14, 1, 1160 Copenhagen, Denmark. SUBSCRIBE: *Kinfolk* is published four times a year. To subscribe, visit kinfolk.com/subscribe or email us at info@kinfolk.com. CONTACT US: If you have questions or comments, please write to us at info@kinfolk.com. For advertising and partnership inquiries, get in touch at advertising@kinfolk.com.

HOUSE OF FINN JUHL

JAPAN SOFA | 1957

finnjuhl.com

WELCOME
The Future Issue

A decade ago, the very first issue of *Kinfolk* made its way into print. Our debut cover featured a simple cup of coffee and a pastry. The issue that you hold in your hands, which celebrates our tenth anniversary, features an image from a futuristic fashion shoot that took place several thousands of miles away from the magazine's natal Portland. The world has changed dramatically since 2011, and *Kinfolk* has changed with it.

To celebrate this milestone, we've refreshed the design of the magazine. The cover will already have struck you as different—so long, white space—but there are exciting changes inside as well: custom typefaces, as well as new feature formats, layouts and contributors. Although the days of flat-lay latte photography are long gone (in *Kinfolk* at least—we take no responsibility for your Instagram feed), some things have held true across the years. In the editors' letter of Issue One, we wrote, "Our goal is for each issue to be an inspiring and reflective experience for each contributor and reader involved." For our decennial edition, we're turning our gaze to a subject that is sure to trigger life's deepest and most searching questions: the future.

Our themed section includes an interview with Sara Seager, an astrophysicist who has dedicated her career to looking for life out in the universe; a report on the CGI models changing the face of the fashion industry; and a creative take on *chindōgu*—the futuristic Japanese gadgets that cause more problems than they solve. On page 150, we commissioned artist Juan Pantoja to design flags to symbolize the values that have underpinned our editorial approach over the last decade and that will carry us into the new one: Wonder, Unity, Openness, Equity and Patience. And, on page 164, we asked five future-focused thinkers what the world might look like in 50 years. Their wildly divergent predictions are a timely reminder that no one can say for certain what's in store.

Of course, we already knew this: If the pandemic has taught us one thing, it's that even the near future can't be anticipated with any degree of accuracy. But the last 18 months have also reinforced our awareness of the fact that family, friends, tight-knit neighborhoods and supportive communities are a bulwark against even the most unimaginable eventualities.

In 2011, the founders of *Kinfolk* would never have predicted that the magazine would survive a decade. It is only through the strength of our own community that we have arrived at Issue Forty. We'd like to thank you sincerely for your enduring support, engagement and inspiration. We can only hope to still be connecting with you on this page in another 10 years.

WORDS
JOHN CLIFFORD BURNS
HARRIET FITCH LITTLE

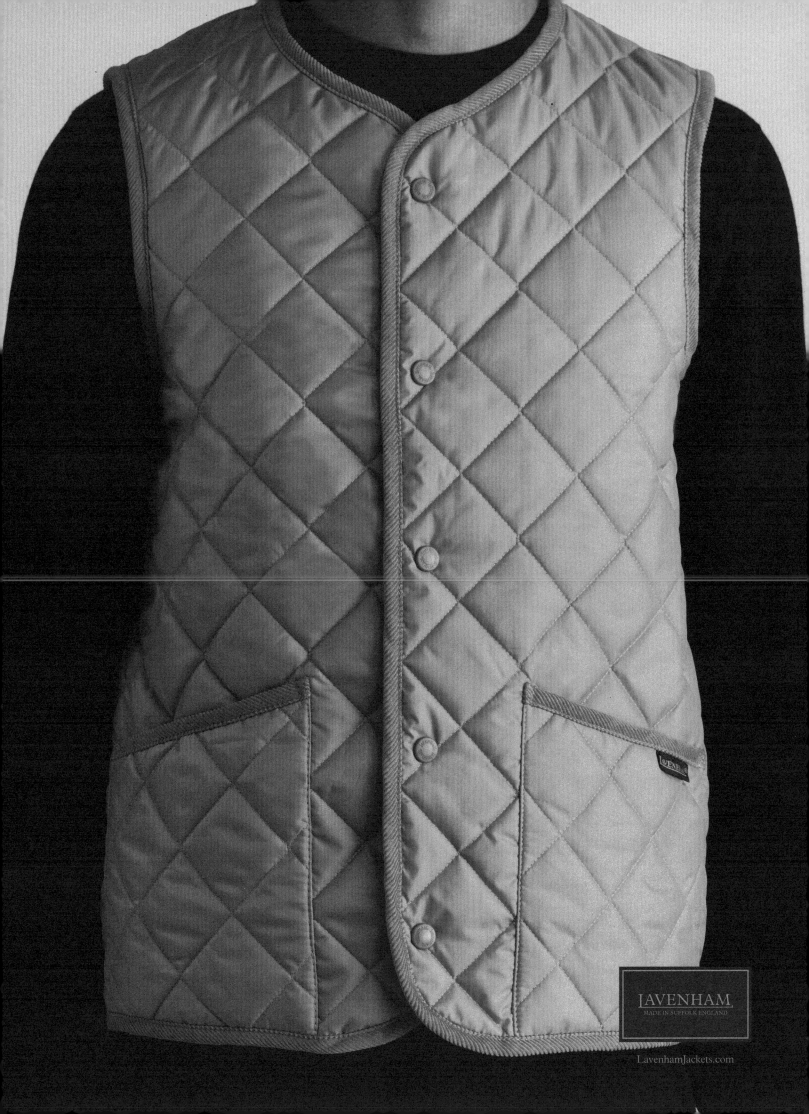

STARTERS
Short answers to big questions.

16 — 48

16	Deep Time Funk		32	Word: Hygiene Theater
20	Lauren Nikrooz		34	Two Doors Down
22	Imitation Gains		36	Olalekan Jeyifous
24	Space Junk		40	Chow Mein & Jello
26	Get Rick Quick		41	Meal in a Pill
30	My Word		42	Mixed Metaphors
31	Good Vibes Only		46	Katie Paterson

FEATURES
Culture from three continents.

50 — 112

50	Fan Bingbing		90	Home Tour: Lucinda Chambers
60	Fractured Frequencies		98	Fan the Flames
70	At Work With: Maniera Gallery		102	Kevin Abstract
78	Lido Pimienta		—	—

"Having a son has tuned me into time in a different way." (Katie Paterson – P. 48)

Photograph: Emman Montalvan

"*I believe in creating the future that you want to live in.*" (Cameron-James Wilson – P. 157)

CONTENTS

114 — 176

FUTURE
A curious guide to the unknown.

114	Earth 2.0	156	Report: The Diigitals
130	Do the Robot	160	Archive: Bodys Isek Kingelez
138	The End Games	164	A Survey of the Future
142	Sara Seager	168	Patent Pending
150	Future Flags	—	—

178 — 192

DIRECTORY
Closing thoughts—and a crossword.

178	Peer Review	186	Crossword
179	Object Matters	187	Correction
180	Cult Rooms	189	Last Night
182	Beverly Glenn-Copeland	190	Credits
184	Bad Idea	191	Stockists
185	Good Idea	192	My Favorite Thing

Photograph: Michael Oliver Love

Born in 1949. Thousands of new configurations yet to be discovered.

string®

String Shelving System configured by interior designer Lotta Agaton. Discovered in 2021.

Part 1.
STARTERS
On buffets, bad neighbors and sci-fi Brooklyn.
16 — 48

16	Deep Time Funk	32	Word: Hygiene Theater
20	Lauren Nikrooz	34	Two Doors Down
22	Imitation Gains	36	Olalekan Jeyifous
24	Space Junk	40	Chow Mein & Jello
26	Get Rick Quick	41	Meal in a Pill
30	My Word	42	Mixed Metaphors
31	Good Vibes Only	46	Katie Paterson

16

DEEP TIME FUNK
How to think in millennia.

The builders of Stonehenge five millennia ago revered the long cycles of time. Their monument measured the annual rhythms of the sun from equinox to equinox and the subtle 18.6-year oscillations of the rising moon. Through a hundred generations, they revised and recalibrated their circles of earth and stone to bind their lives with celestial time.

A world away, under the tropical sun, Mayans identified their place in time within expansive overlapping patterns of days. Their Long Count calendar encompassed cycles that stretched 5,000 years, from the primordial origins of life to the imponderable beginnings of a new era.

Our own highly regulated time never seems so expansive. We live in tight temporal patterns. These begin with a momentary, global celebration that rolls from New Zealand to Alaska on New Year's Eve and provokes a crucial modern ritual: tossing out one calendar and replacing it with another. This new calendar, minutely subdivided into months, weeks, days, and ever-smaller increments, controls our frenetic lives. To function properly, we must attune ourselves to these fine-grained cadences. Failure to fall in step can lead to deep malaise, even mental disorder—one form of schizophrenia results from what psychologists Kai Vogeley and Christian Kupke term "a structural disturbance of time consciousness." It is hard not to feel a touch of this disturbance in our day-to-day lives.

To counter the short-term thinking that accompanies this dominant perception of time, a group of cultural pioneers—Danny Hillis, Stewart Brand and Brian Eno—founded the Long Now Foundation in 1996. One of its most intriguing projects is the 10,000 Year Clock, currently undergoing a slow process of construction in the desert of western Texas.[1] Its designer, Hillis, first proposed "a clock that ticks once a year. The century hand advances every 100 years, and the cuckoo comes out on the millennium." Running off a trickle of energy captured from daily temperature changes and occasional boosts of human energy supplied by visitors, the clock will span the life of our civilization. Its creators hope that by stepping into the clock's long flow of time, visitors will remember to participate in slower rhythms.

The Scottish artist Katie Paterson, interviewed on page 46, creates work that "collapses the distance between the viewer and the most distant edges of time." Her recordings of melting glaciers, photographs of darkness in interstellar space and assembly of clocks attuned to other planets, all reach out from the mundane to open new frames of reference.

These projects remind us that we do not need to bind ourselves exclusively to the agitated rhythms of modern life, and challenge us to reactivate the primordial, expansive, life-affirming cycles of time.

WORDS
ALEX ANDERSON
PHOTO
KATYA MUKHINA

(1) Another of the foundation's projects is Long Bets, an organization through which people can bet money on future eventualities, with the winnings going to charity. Bets currently open include that by 2030 people will routinely fly in pilotless planes, that by 2050 slaughterhouses will be banned in the UK, and that by 2060 there will be fewer humans on the planet than there are today.

SMELLS LIKE TEAM SPIRIT
A three-step guide to pep talks.

WORDS
BELLA GLADMAN
PHOTO
MICHAEL OLIVER LOVE

Once more unto the breach! A pep talk, if done well, can inspire an army into battle. *Go get 'em* also works in less dramatic circumstances. Research by Professor Tiffanye Vargas at California State University shows that, across sports, coaches' pre-game speeches matter: 90% of players enjoy listening, and 65% say pep talks affect the way they play. Business leaders, too, have focused on how to best motivate their employees. According to research by husband-and-wife team Jacqueline and Milton Mayfield, a good pep talk includes clear directions, empathetic language and an explanation of why a task is important to you and the wider community. Depending on the audience, the weighting of each element can vary. For example, if you're encouraging a friend, you might not need to establish empathy as much as you would if you were rallying strangers. And when *you're* the person who needs some motivation, writer Josh Gondelman recommends giving a pep talk to a buddy. After all, in passing on inspirational words, you too might take in the message.
—

Sets that Nikrooz has devised include a walk-in freezer (for Selena Gomez's "Fetish") and a full fairground (for Travis Scott's "Antidote").

LAUREN NIKROOZ

WORDS
AVA WONG DAVIES
PHOTO
EMMA TRIM

Four questions for a set designer.

New York–based production and set designer Lauren Nikrooz has racked up an eclectic portfolio of clients over the last 10 years, with projects ranging from Travis Scott music videos to Dior ad campaigns and Marina Abramović's film work for MoMA. Nikrooz, who is of British and Persian heritage, trained at art school in Manchester and at London's Royal Academy of Dramatic Art (RADA) before moving to the US. Her designs radiate the kind of offhand, nostalgic elegance that is often approvingly described as "editorial"—more focused on cultivating a specific mood than on showcasing products.

AVA WONG DAVIES: You studied design at drama school. How has the theater influenced your practice?

LAUREN NIKROOZ: It's scrappy, and it makes you think on your feet. RADA was hard work because you would always be training in something different, like costume, or scenic painting, or set design. I didn't want to focus on production design at the time because I just wanted to be an artist, but they made you do it and it was so good for me. It trained me in how to do something practically, not just creatively. Nowadays, I always have to consider what effect a decision I make might have on the other departments I'm working with.

AWD: What role does improvisation play in your work?

LN: There have definitely been times when I've come up with something in advance that I really thought was going to work, but on the day I might realize that a certain carpet actually looks better than the flooring I'd planned. That's the fun bit, when you can play around with all that stuff. I feel like my adrenaline is always at a thousand miles per hour.

AWD: What's the most difficult prop you've had to source?

LN: On a job for Calvin Klein, I found a spiral staircase—this beautiful mid-century modern piece. I had never put a spiral staircase on the set of anything before, so I'm really glad we did it. But it was a huge job. We needed everyone in the grip department and the art department to set it up because it was metal, and so heavy. You only catch a tiny glimpse of it in the finished photos, but that's always how it goes.

AWD: Is there a common misconception people have about your job?

LN: People assume it's really glamorous, but we wrapped a job last night and it was crazy. We had a bunch of locations, 12 models, and at the end of the day we had three trucks and loads of cargo because we'd been set-dressing all these houses. The art director took a photo of the whole situation, and it just looked like a really messy car boot sale. By contrast, my house is very sculptural and sparse. I'm a minimalist at home, but I can barely open the door to my studio.

IMITATION GAINS
On the benefits of artificial greenery.

The idea that getting out to the country is good for our health is as old as medicine itself. Modern science seems to bear out the idea, with a host of studies demonstrating the therapeutic effects of exposure to nature. Japanese scientists have demonstrated that long walks in the woods produce lower levels of cortisol—a hormone linked to stress—and reduce blood pressure.

As to why nature makes us feel better, the verdict is still out. In 1984, biologist E.O. Wilson proposed the "biophilia" theory, which suggests that we evolved to prefer the sight of resource-rich environments— the blue of clean water, the green of fertile fields and forests—and that this has led to a salutary neural response.

On a gut level, many of us feel that organic things are just ineffably better than their synthetic or inert counterparts. Woe betide the pretenders: plastic houseplants, dyed flowers, Astroturf and bad CGI.

But what if our assumption—that "organic" nature is inherently better—is wrong to begin with? Nothing, after all, is genuinely unnatural. Video games and Netflix entertain us with the same photons as a campfire. Every psychotropic drug is derived from substances and chemical processes provided by the good old universe itself. What we mean by "unnatural" is that human beings have stirred the pot. But if something can make us happier, or healthier, what's the difference?

Research is beginning to turn up some interesting answers. Studies have shown that nature-based virtual reality experiences can alleviate anxiety and pain in hospital patients, and can even lead to quicker recovery times. Russian dairy cows produced better milk after being fitted with VR headsets that simulated a summer field. By way of anecdote, this writer derived considerable solace from a cheap star projector that painted the cosmos on his apartment's ceiling during quarantine in New York.

We live in an urbanizing world where access to real nature is often a privilege, and in which nature itself is under persistent threat from man-made causes. There will never be a replacement for the woods at dusk, nor for the eerie waver of a loon's call. But in some cases, embracing the simulation will do. And there may be a lot of making do ahead.

WORDS
ASHER ROSS
PHOTO
ROMAIN LAPRADE

FELLOW FEELING
The pleasure of a stranger's touch.

WORDS
BAYA SIMONS
PHOTO
OYE DIRAN

In Teju Cole's novel *Open City*, Julius, the Nigerian doctor whom we follow as he wanders around Manhattan, describes going to a tailor's shop. "For me, the intimate wonder of getting measured for clothes was like that of getting your hair cut, or feeling the warm touch of the doctor's hand nestled against your throat as he took your temperature," he writes. "These were the rare cases in which you gave permission to a stranger to enter your personal space." His tentative "for me" reveals the unspoken nature of the pleasure that's found in the touch of a stranger; as if admitting so exposes a lack of intimacy in the rest of our lives.

But it is a common pleasure. The pseudoscientific phenomenon of ASMR (autonomous sensory meridian response, the brain-tingling feeling caused by certain sounds and experiences) points to its appeal. Videos promising to deliver the trademark sensation, which can be triggered by everything from being checked into a hotel by a soft-voiced receptionist to receiving a cranial nerve exam, have racked up hundreds of millions of views online. Indeed, the experiences described in *Open City*—visiting the tailor, the doctor, the hairdresser— are some of the most popular categories of role-play in ASMR content.

The British neuroscientist Francis Mc-Glone advanced a convincing explanation. His research shows that humans have nerve receptors known as C-tactile afferents that produce pleasure when stimulated. Significantly, they're located not in erogenous zones, but on the head, face, arms and back. Scientists refer to the pleasure we get from these nerves as "social touch."[1] A psychoanalytic reading would suggest that we chase this sensation because it recalls how we were soothed as babies.

But why do we crave physical contact with strangers—not just with our loved ones? In an essay on touch in Chinese culture for the journal *Granta*, Poppy Sebag-Montefiore suggests a cultural explanation for the desire. She posits that the West lacks a culture of social touch as it currently exists in China, where she describes seeing strangers freely resting on each other in queues. Perhaps this need for social connection that's free from the complexities of sex is what we're seeking to fill with ASMR, haircuts and visits to the tailor: the urge to feel kinship with the world around us.

(1) In the animal kingdom, this is known as allogrooming. The gelada baboon spends 17% of its day engaged in grooming or being groomed—far more than is necessary for the sake of hygiene alone.

SPACE JUNK

WORDS
SALA ELISE PATTERSON

In conversation with a space archaeologist.

Humans have left about 34,000 objects in space. Some are predictable (satellites), others not (discarded zip ties, and Elon Musk's personal Tesla Roadster). Dr. Alice Gorman is a space archaeologist who is fascinated by this "space junk" and what it tells us about humanity and our future. Gorman began her career studying Aboriginal archaeology in her native Australia. Contemplation of the sky one night in 2002 led to an epiphany: Space is full of orbital junk with an archaeological record and heritage value. These days, Gorman goes by Dr. Space Junk. In her new book, *Dr Space Junk vs The Universe: Archaeology and the Future*, she allows us to consider the final frontier through a different lens.

SALA ELISE PATTERSON: What meaning does archaeology take on in space?

ALICE GORMAN: The same thing it would on a site that was one million years old. I look at how humans interact with objects and environments and observe large-scale patterns of behavior and change over time. I'm interested in what it is about space, technology and the different environments of, say, being in microgravity in Earth's orbit that shape the way humans move and the relationships they have with objects and technologies. It's about understanding human behavior in space but also looking at what goes on in space as a way of getting a new perspective on how humans operate on Earth.

SEP: Is the common perception that humanity will have a fresh start in space confirmed by what you are observing?

AG: This belief that space will erase the inequalities and conflicts we see on Earth is charming, but people don't act differently in space. I'm looking at the International Space Station, for example, and how things have been constructed without female bodies in mind. There is a relationship between the type of architecture you live in and the social relations that are produced. I've not seen any indication that people are thinking outside the Western capitalist nuclear family [model]. So, taking the archaeological perspective, I don't see any indications that it's going to be better in space.

SEP: Do humans treat space with respect?

AG: The assumption I've seen expressed is a very 15th-century view that non-living systems are resources for humans to use and have mastery over. There's a completely different sensibility now around the idea that the resources on Earth only exist for human use. There hasn't really been, until recently, any consideration of space as an environment with some kind of value in its own right that has a right to exist outside of human use.

SEP: How are we thinking about environmental protection when it comes to space?

AG: The dominant approach to looking at space junk is less about the impacts on the space environment and more about the impacts on humans using it. My archaeological perspective instead asks: What is this new space environment? What is the combination of all the stuff humans have put up there with all the preexisting conditions, natural objects and cosmic dust? We can only answer by getting samples of that dust, working out how much of it is human stuff, how it's changing, what Earth elements are creeping into the dust of outer space, and by tracking changes to the environment over time. Looking at how human materials are contributing to a completely different type of space environment as a creative process is a different perspective that is very interesting to me.

—

25

WORDS
DEBIKA RAY
PHOTO
ROMAIN LAPRADE

Early retirement has had a catchy rebrand. The Financial Independence, Retire Early movement—FIRE, for short—popularized over the past decade or so by such books as *Your Money or Your Life* by Vicki Robin and Joe Dominguez and *The Simple Path to Wealth* by JL Collins, as well as countless blogs—is a community of people who seek to opt out of employment in their 30s or 40s by making as much money and spending as little as possible for a few, intense years.

The idea is to accumulate enough savings to be able to live off the passive income for the rest of your life. Advocates suggest you need to bank 25 times your planned annual spending before quitting, and then withdraw just 4% of your portfolio each year. This means saving aggressively—up to 75% of your earnings—and cutting your living costs down to a minimum, with the assumption that your frugal habits will persist. Pete Adeney, author of the *Mr. Money Mustache* blog, who retired before 30, offers prescriptions including "Ride a bike wherever you can," "Lose the overpriced cell phones," and "Learn to mock convenience."[1]

But whichever way you cut it, the movement is inescapably elitist—you need a substantial income to even contemplate saving the amounts necessary to live out this plan, not to mention the fact that joblessness and the pursuit of pleasure come with stigma for most social groups. The plan is also inherently individualistic. In its reliance on highly paid jobs and investments, it calls for an alternative lifestyle without upturning the social framework it springs from. "From what I've seen, a lot of people seem to be selling it as a philosophy, but the philosophy basically seems to be, 'be rich,'" says David Frayne, sociologist and author of the book *The Refusal of Work*, whose research centers

around the possibilities of a more collectivist post-work society. "There doesn't seem to be much acknowledgment of the role of privilege or luck."

At the heart of the movement is a desire to be unchained from the constraints of unsatisfactory paid employment and being defined by your career—a desire that isn't uncommon, even if unattainable for most. Frayne discovered a similar motivation in his interviews with people who had rejected work as a political project. "They weren't committed to idleness, but to the idea of doing meaningful work—something that does good or allows you to stretch your capacities," he says. "We tend to think of social contribution in terms of employment, but there's a host of valuable things people can do outside their jobs, from artistic work to political activism."

Over the past year, ideas such as a shorter working week and universal basic income have gained mainstream popularity, as the coronavirus pandemic has forced us to rethink what activities we consider essential and to pay attention to how precarious so many jobs are. In there lies a glimmer of hope of a society in which security, agency, choice and fulfillment—goals that followers of the FIRE movement seek for themselves—might be within reach for us all.

(1) A striking proportion of people who do manage to retire young then dedicate their time to teaching others how to follow suit with books, courses and speeches. Conveniently, most of these activities generate further income—which raises the question of how financially independent some FIRE retirees really are.

Architecture: Richard England

GET RICH QUICK
The illusion of the FIRE movement.

IN SEASON
Potable water meets palatable design.

Photograph: Risto Kamunen, 1968

In functional terms, a water tower is just about the most uninspiring piece of construction imaginable. Ubiquitous and enormous, they are used to create the pressure that pumps water into local taps, showerheads and swimming pools. But these hulking storage units have become a surprise success story of municipal architecture. Perhaps because of the way they define horizons, water towers invite the fanciful imagination of architects and planners. American water towers have often taken on novelty shapes (corncobs, ketchup bottles, pineapples) while modern architects have built new towers with bold lines—a phenomenon faithfully documented by mid-century photographers Hilla and Bernd Becher, who published a whole photo book, *Anonymous Sculptures*, dedicated to water towers and other industrial architecture.

Why do we like them so much? Joan Didion described her awe at the civil engineering involved in California's water system in her 1977 essay *Holy Water*, and indeed water towers fulfill the fascination with grand designs that humans have had since the Tower of Babel. Being community projects rather than luxury buildings, however, water towers have escaped the phallocentric hubris that skyscrapers have acquired over the years. They are human-made and civic minded, but still capable of inspiring awe.

WORDS
BELLA GLADMAN

Falstaff was a master of the imaginative curse. In *Henry IV, Part I*, the wayward knight calls Prince Hal and others starvelings, whoreson caterpillars, bacon-fed knaves, and bull's pizzles.

To many, Falstaff is just the sort of individual one might expect to curse so often and well: crude and hot-tempered, an inveterate drunkard and all-around scoundrel. But what if swearing weren't the mark of an impoverished character or intellect, but rather the sign of a great communicator? According to Melissa Mohr, author of *Holy Shit: A Brief History of Swearing*, letting loose with the occasional expletive is an excellent way of communicating meaning. When you swear at someone, *really* swear at them, that person knows you're deadly serious. When you unleash a string of four-letter words after slamming your hand in a car door, folks know it really hurts. A good curse word or five lets people know how you feel, and just how intense that feeling is. "The most potent words of all—the ones that have a direct line to the emotions—are profanity," Mohr writes in her 2010 book. "Name a feeling, and profanity can elicit it."

And cursing is hardly the refuge of the unimaginative and the vocabulary-deficient. As it turns out, many of the bluest talkers have the greatest reserves of words to draw from. In a 2015 study conducted by Timothy Jay, author of *Cursing in America*, researchers found that people who could come up with the most animal names in 60 seconds were also able to come up with the most swear words. "A voluminous taboo lexicon may better be considered an indicator of healthy verbal abilities rather than a cover for their deficiencies," the study concluded.

In addition to showing off your language mastery—as spoken-word poets do, and competitive Scrabble players—and letting friends know just how you feel, swearing is also good for your health. Research studies have shown that cursing can make you stronger (subjects that swore before riding exercise bikes went harder than those who did not), and better able to endure discomfort (having your hand submerged in ice water, for example).[1] So let loose on your best pal! Your body and spirit will thank you, even if your friend does not.

(1) These studies overturned the previously dominant assumption that swearing was a "maladaptive" response to pain that made us feel things more rather than less.

WORDS
ROBERT ITO
PHOTO
CHARLOTTE LAPALUS

MY WORD
In praise of cursing.

One of the more perverse features of social media is that it often produces the opposite of its stated intentions. It claims to bring us closer together; it leaves us divided and angry. It professes to be a transmitter of knowledge; it has convinced your grandfather that Bill Gates is Satan incarnate. And, while social media aims to be a supportive space, its relentless cheeriness often curdles into something sinister—a monomaniacal valorization of *good vibes* above all else. Now, there's a term for this singular pursuit of uplifting feeling via Instagram captions that forbid "bad energy" and "the haters": toxic positivity.

Toxic positivity did not come from the internet. But its place in the popular consciousness is inextricable from the web. Google searches for the term first rose in February 2019 and exploded in 2020, a year of mass suffering and mental angst, with *Vogue*, *The Cut*, the *Huffington Post* and *Refinery29* all weighing in. *Vogue* identified in particular the knee-jerk calls to cheer up that emerge whenever someone expresses negative emotions on the internet: "Going through a breakup? *You'll find someone else!*" The task of honoring one's feelings—difficult or joyful—requires intimacy, generosity, mutual trust and freedom from shame. These feel far from the dominant features of social media, a place where people go to prove to an indeterminate public they're doing very well, actually. No wonder any attempts to instill cheer feel insincere—just another punitive standard against which we will all fall short.

And like anything on the web today, the true beneficiaries of toxic positivity are the wealthy and powerful. A celebrity can use it to deflect criticism from hosting a party during the pandemic; marketing departments have found that "You go girl!" is a better slogan to print on an "empowering" water bottle than "I hear your pain and stand with you." (Toxic positivity tends to be feminized; the masculine equivalent is the cooler-than-you alpha voice that demands that you "not be a dick.")

But the vulnerable and suffering—and even those just having a bad day—don't need platitudes (nor the empowering water bottle). They need to be held. Perhaps the best "positivity" of all is one that accepts difficult emotions as a fact of life and ensures that they are listened to and processed—preferably in the company of other people who share in your pain, rather than drown it out with a series of can-do mottoes.

WORDS
REBECCA LIU

Photograph: *Saul Steinberg, New York 1978* by Evelyn Hofer

GOOD VIBES ONLY
A primer on toxic positivity.

WORD: HYGIENE THEATER
On the stagecraft of sanitization.

WORDS
PRECIOUS ADESINA
PHOTO
TOM HARTFORD

Etymology: In 2010, journalist James Fallows coined the term "security theater" in an article for *The Atlantic*, referring to measures put in place after the 9/11 attacks to give the general public a heightened sense of security. According to Derek Thompson, a colleague of Fallows, the coronavirus outbreak has generated similar performative behavior surrounding cleanliness. Writing in *The Atlantic* in July 2020, he borrowed Fallows' phrase and dubbed it "hygiene theater."

Meaning: There are many things in life that have little or no purpose other than giving us reassurance: the sound of a car door slamming closed, the whir of a cash machine, the shutter noise of a smartphone camera. The same techniques are also used to offer a sense of security during the darkest of times.

The simple airport security pat-down, which grew increasingly more frequent after 9/11, would need to be far more thorough to eradicate a potential threat. But sometimes the pressure to seem as if the correct procedures are in place trumps their actual utility. "Otherwise, we'd never fly—or would strip everyone nude before boarding, do cavity searches, and carry no cargo," Fallows wrote.

Since the beginning of the coronavirus outbreak, the airport pat-down has taken on a new form. Around the world, there has been an emphasis on deep cleaning. An "extensive cleaning regime" has become marketing 101 within the hospitality industry. (The White House is reported to have had a deep clean worth half a million dollars before the Biden administration moved in.)[1]

But according to an article in the medical journal *The Lancet* in July 2020, the research suggesting that COVID remains on surfaces for days is based on exaggerated laboratory circumstances; around 100 people would need to sneeze on the same part of a surface for the same conditions to be replicated in the outside world. Meanwhile, evidence has consistently shown that it's poorly ventilated spaces that pose the highest risk of infection.

The problem is that whoever decides to remove these superficial efforts also has to be willing to take the blame if something goes wrong. Who wants to be the first one to tell people to stop wiping surfaces, and potentially be held responsible for another tragedy? The pandemic will pass, but it seems the smell of disinfectant will linger on.

(1) During the 2021 US presidential inauguration, an assistant was tasked with disinfecting the podium in between every speech. The "sanitizer in chief" was granted his 15 minutes of fame on Twitter, where he was praised for cleaning away the former administration's "bad vibes."

33

TWO DOORS DOWN
When good neighbors go online.

Artwork: *Night* by George Underwood

In the early days of the COVID-19 pandemic, one positive sentiment gained traction: that despite the harsh new realities of physical distancing, we were "closer" to each other than we'd ever been before. This optimistic paradox emerged from the observation that neighbors were rallying together—whether singing from balconies, or connecting through online networks of support and mutual aid.

Hyperlocal online groups didn't start with the coronavirus, but they certainly rose to new heights with it. Usage of Nextdoor, a global social network for local communities, jumped in March 2020, and informal networks sprang up through Whatsapp and Facebook. Members used them to check in on the lonely and vulnerable, organize shopping and medicine pick-ups and exchange goods.

It was to be expected that these interactions would drop off somewhat as people adapted to pandemic life. The surprise was that, often, the group dynamics also soured. Users witnessed feuds, surveillance and shaming, sometimes involving photos of people posted without their permission (an intrusion that has only been made easier by the normalization of doorbell cameras). In majority white neighborhoods, such incidents have often involved the racial profiling of perceived "outsiders"—a problem that took on a new guise in summer 2020 when several Nextdoor local moderators deleted and censored pro–Black Lives Matter posts. Apparently, giving moderation duties to the first person who registers a group might not be the best approach to inclusive community-building after all. Nextdoor is looking at recruiting more representative team leads, and in the meantime has introduced bias training and removed direct connections to law enforcement.

Beyond the incidents that involve clear racial prejudice, there are certain patterns to online behavior that help to explain the recurring hostility. One is that it's an environment where outrage thrives. A 2017 study by researchers at New York University found that each moral or emotional word in a Tweet increases the likelihood of it being retweeted by 20%. That means that Nextdoor posts involving COVID-shaming and leaf-blower wars are more likely to be engaged with, seen and shared.

Other explanations are perennial. Community groups have long been about who is excluded as much as who is included. Pressuring those who are included to toe the line is a way of maintaining that boundary.

For all the utility of online networks, there's reason to look forward to the return of offline neighborliness, with its default politeness and serendipity. Even Nextdoor CEO Sarah Friar has previously admitted that, whereas other social networks try to keep you hooked in, for her company to be doing well its users shouldn't spend too much time online.

WORDS
RIMA SABINA AOUF

OLALEKAN JEYIFOUS

WORDS
KYLA MARSHELL
PHOTO
OUMAYMA B. TANFOUS

On fantastical architecture and sci-fi Brooklyn.

There Are Black People in the Future. So goes a phrase coined by artist Alisha B. Wormsley. It's a provocative statement, in part because it seems both obvious—why wouldn't Black people exist in the future?—and interested in challenging the notion that they might not. For Olalekan Jeyifous, a Brooklyn-based architect and artist, the question of where Black people might exist, both geographically and otherwise, resides squarely at the center of his work. In both large-scale public art and speculative architecture, he imagines other worlds, sometimes layered right on top of this one, and what the spaces we occupy say about us and society.

KYLA MARSHELL: Your work has been described as futurist, or Afrofuturist. Do you identify as such?

OLALEKAN JEYIFOUS: Not really; but I'm not offended by these terms. I don't mind labels at all. Anything that'll give someone access to the kind of work that I do, I'm pretty much cool with. I would say less futurist because sometimes, when I'm creating what I'm creating, it doesn't necessarily need to exist in the future. I'd say my work is much more science fiction. Right now, a lot of my stuff employs kind of fantastical green and sustainable technologies. So it's not always that I'm operating in the future, but definitely on a kind of alternate timeline in order to examine contemporary issues.

KM: Is your work a way of imagining Black people in the future, or imagining space for Black people?

OJ: Yes, absolutely. For this exhibit I'm in at the Museum of Modern Art, *Reconstructions: Architecture and Blackness in America*, I'm imagining a kind of postindustrial, post-capitalist, pre-gentrified Brooklyn. I set up parameters around this world. The premise is that global warming and climate change reach a very critical point of crisis in, like, 1972. And the government enacts a series of policies [including] where individuals are granted a certain amount of mobility credits, to curtail travel and all of the greenhouse gas emissions that occur through that. So I imagine it's a free market and rich people buy a lot of the mobility credits somehow. And so poorer neighborhoods are left without mobility credits and effectively become kind of frozen in space, or at least contained within their communities. And then what comes out of that world? I haven't spelled out what year it is in the exhibit, but a lot of the imagery is a mix of things from now or the late 1970s and mid-1990s.

KM: Can architecture solve problems of structural inequality on its own? Or do larger systems—housing, for example—need to be addressed first?

OJ: Architecture in and of itself can't solve anything, particularly when architecture is just another institution. That's almost like saying, "Can this drug, or this vaccine do away with the health disparities that we have in the Black community?" And the answer is no, because it's controlled by a system. Every single level controls who gets that drug—how much it costs, who has access to it. So there's an entire complicated ecosystem of racism that reinforces all those repressive aspects, and every single institution in the entire country and world falls within that system—health, education, architecture, whatever. I do think that there is good design; it can definitely function to alleviate certain things. But I think those things don't occur on a macro scale.

—

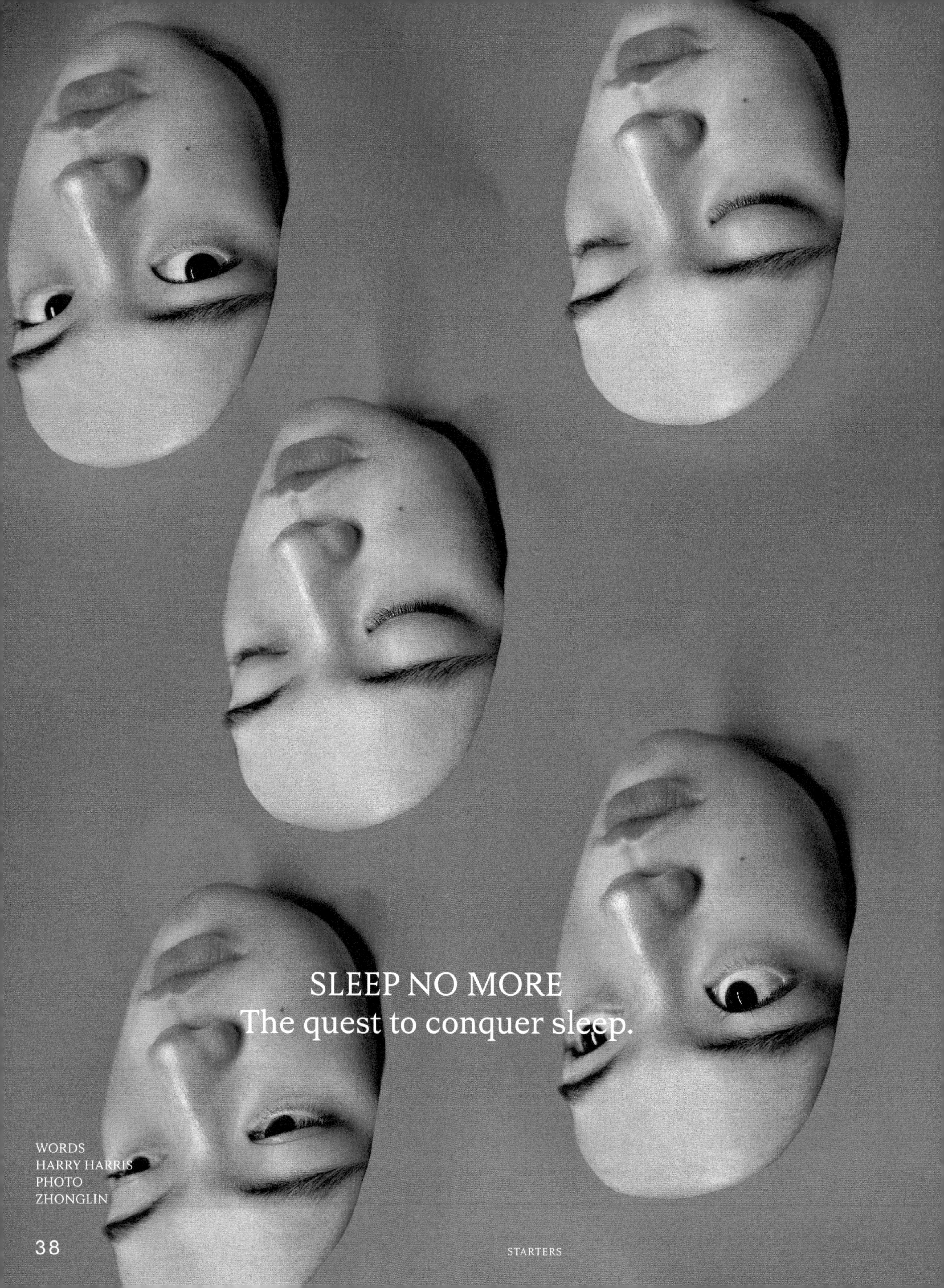

SLEEP NO MORE
The quest to conquer sleep.

WORDS
HARRY HARRIS
PHOTO
ZHONGLIN

We are sleeping less than ever. In 2018, researchers from Ball State University looked at data from over 150,000 adults between 2010 and 2018 and found that the prevalence of "inadequate" sleep—defined as seven hours or less—had risen from 30.9% to 35.6%. Since the industrial revolution, the typical working day has been divided into three equal parts: work, free time and sleep. As we have become more connected, our lives more fast-paced, sleep is the sacrificial third.

Could this be the beginning of the end, not just for the eight-hour workday, but for sleep as the great unifier? For years, armed forces have experimented with drugging their soldiers to keep them awake—from British soldiers mainlining tea in World War I to Americans in Vietnam consuming so-called "pep pills," generally the amphetamine Dexedrine. More recently, a drug called modafinil has been experimented with by armies in India, China, South Korea, France, the UK and the US. Its function? To enable people to perform at their peak without the need for sleep.

Military innovations often seep into society—duct tape, freeze drying and GPS all have their origins in army requirements. If the quest to conquer soldiers' need for sleep is successful, it will likely not be contained within a military orbit for long. Author Jonathan Crary suggests that "the sleepless soldier would be the forerunner of the sleepless worker or consumer." In fact, modafinil is already prescribed to civilians to treat conditions including narcolepsy and shift work sleep disorder.

But will conquering sleep make us more productive, more creative, better workers?[1] Archimedes had his "Eureka!" moment while resting in the bath. Paul McCartney said the melody for "Yesterday" came to him in a dream. Cognitive psychologist Scott Barry Kaufman found that 72% of people get creative ideas in the shower—the relaxed state it creates being conducive to inspiration. It may be tempting to think that the only barrier to our progress is the amount of hours in the day, but by working more, we are potentially losing out on far more than just sleep.

(1) Another ill-fated attempt to conquer sleep is the Uberman schedule, in which you take six 20-minute naps over the course of each 24-hour period. Studies have shown that not only is polyphasic sleep extremely disruptive to a body's natural circadian rhythm, but that it is associated with poorer academic performance—even compared to people who have slept the same short number of hours in one stretch.

CHOW MEIN & JELLO
An ode to the buffet.

In the Disney movie *Aladdin*, when our charming hero steps into the Cave of Wonders, he's gobsmacked by the sheer physical volume of the wealth inside. Piles of riches five times his height spill onto the cave floor. "Wouldja look at that?" the young rapscallion remarks to his pet monkey. While most people now keep their money in the bank rather than in subterranean desert caverns, there is a modern experience equivalent to Aladdin's fantastical first glimpse into the Cave of Wonders: the buffet.

Today's buffet displays run the gamut from the chic platters of pomegranate-studded grain salads at Ottolenghi in North London to the cheap and cheerful $9.99 all-you-can-eat weekday spread at Angie's Buffet in Heber Springs, Arkansas.

All are characterized by an ungodly amount of food. And the reaction is largely the same, whether the food is piled on hand-thrown ceramics or in industrial-sized aluminum chafing dishes: childlike awe at the opulence, followed by a rush to the stacks of plates.

The appeal of lavish abundance is obvious. Another common buffet behavior is harder to explain: the tendency to make oneself sick with too many plates of penne Alfredo, enchiladas, shrimp tempura, and devil's food cake. Some psychologists believe it has to do with getting our money's worth. When you pay in advance, each trip to the buffet makes the experience seem like better value.

Conspicuous consumption has its downsides: What was luxurious abundance one day is food waste the next.[1] Cruise ships, famous for their sumptuous buffets, pulverize uneaten food and "feed it to the fishes" (read: dump it into the ocean). Las Vegas casinos send uneaten food to Las Vegas Livestock, whose 5,000 pigs easily get through the food waste generated from Aria, Bellagio, Luxor, and the Venetian.

Increasing concerns about sustainability, as well as a trend away from the more-is-more 20th century, have diminished the buffet's popularity. Many who consider the buffet to be déclassé prefer the pretension of "all-you-care-to-eat" dining experiences. But the reaction to dazzling displays of piles of bounty—whether lo mein noodles or golden coins—is inescapably human.

(1) A 2017 study by Ideo found that guests typically eat just over half of the food available at a hotel buffet. Because of hygiene regulations, only 10-15% of the leftovers can be recycled.

WORDS
STEPHANIE D'ARC TAYLOR
PHOTO
AARON TILLEY

Food Styling: Iain Graham. Set Design: Elena Horn

MEAL IN A PILL
On sci-fi's staple diet.

In 1893, the American suffragette and populist Mary E. Lease imagined a world without food. Writing for the American Press Association ahead of the World's Fair in Chicago, she described her utopian vision for the year 1993, where a single plant-based pill could feed a person for days: "And thus the problems of cooks and cooking will be solved." The "problem," as she saw it, wasn't food, but obligatory, time-consuming work. At a time when women were responsible for feeding the household, the meal replacement pill must have seemed a sensible solution to the shackles of domesticity, freeing women to stake their claim to the male-dominated public sphere.

But it wasn't only women who were set to benefit: Lease positioned the pill as a feature of an enlightened society where men and women were equal, three hours constituted "a long day's work" and money hoarders were classed with criminals.

1993 has come and gone, and, while food pills have become a sci-fi trope (see *The Jetsons, Doctor Who, Star Trek,* et al.), the meal-free future Lease imagined hasn't come to pass, and likely never will. And this isn't just because a lot of people seem to like food and dining, nor because science hasn't backed it up.

While not an exact facsimile, meal replacement powders and drinks like Huel and Soylent—which offer all the nutritional value of a meal without the hassle of actually making one—build on Lease's concept of better eating through chemistry.[1] But their proliferation has come to represent the opposite of what she'd intended.

Instead of free time and liberation, meal replacements have become symbols of the macho culture of overwork glorified by Silicon Valley. They're the antithesis of the long lunch, the three-day workweek and the breezy out-of-office message warning that no, you will not be checking your email while on vacation—anything that prioritizes pleasure over productivity.

Time reclaimed from cooking and eating seems poised to be redirected not to leisure and home life, but back into the very labor Lease had hoped to see reduced. Where she went wrong, then, wasn't in imagining a world without traditional food, but a world where free time would be seen as anything more than more potential working hours. Food itself has never been the problem. It's our relationships with leisure and labor that need to be reevaluated.

(1) Huel claims to provide all the vitamins and nutrients the human body needs, but few people are able to stick to its diet of shakes and powders. The texture of food, and its social context, are intrinsic parts of eating.

Photo: *Pratos* by German Lorca

WORDS
ALLYSSIA ALLEYNE

42

MIXED METAPHORS

WORDS
BELLA GLADMAN
PHOTO
PAULA CODONER

Let's get our ducks on the same page.

Retired federal judge Dave Hatfield has been collecting malaphors for over 30 years and posting them on his website, malaphors.com, for nearly 10. Malaphors are mixed metaphors—the product of two idioms blended together to make a humorous Frankenphrase such as: "I'll burn that bridge when I come to it." Though most commonly observed in political punditry and sports commentary on TV and radio, none of us will escape getting our linguistic wires crossed from time to time. Hatfield says that's no bad thing: In fact, it reveals the creative, mutable power of language.

BELLA GLADMAN: You've been collecting malaphors for 30 years. What initially drew you to them?

DAVE HATFIELD: There's a part of me that's drawn to using language creatively. When I used to teach law to new judges, I'd integrate the legal concepts into song, and the information was understood and retained much better! In one of my previous workplaces, there was a gentleman who would use these fractured idioms to the point where I started collecting them. I'm still doing it, as one of my retirement hobbies.

BG: What's kept you interested all this time?

DH: The irreverent humor. And while some malaphors are fairly common, because of the word association, "I heard it off the top of my cuff," for example—a mix of "off the top of my head" and "off the cuff"—it seems like malaphors are endless. I've got a universe of folks that hear them on television or radio shows and send them to me.

BG: Why are malaphors so common in the media?

DH: When you have a lot of folks ad-libbing on television, they have got a lot of time to fill, and the English language has tended, over the years, toward cliché. Malaphors tend to come up when you're yakking extemporaneously. A good example is Donald Trump, who would go off script a lot. As a society, we are pontificating more. The mind is searching for something to say, and what actually gets activated is something different. For instance, with the question "What do cows drink?" 99% of people think of milk first. It's like the mind is reaching into a cookie jar, and picking out the broken pieces of two different cookies.

BG: What if you're not a native English speaker?

DH: When I first started the website, I had a couple of folks write to me from other countries, including a gentleman from France who taught English as a foreign language. He thought the site was a good device to teach English and asked if I could define the actual idioms that were being mixed, for purposes of instruction—and that's what I do now. In terms of having English as a second language, it might be that you make a mistake with an idiom, rather than muddling two together.

BG: Are people who use malaphors likely to be talking out of their proverbial behind?

DH: I don't think so. Malaphor usage seems to run across all lines of education and situations, and they are very unintentional and buried in the recesses of the mind. Malaprops, though, that's a different matter. Malaprop is the misuse of a word, and that's more likely to be attempting to be highfalutin, trying to use a word that they really don't know the meaning for, like *My grandfather came over to America vis-à-vis Canada*, instead of *via Canada*. Sometimes malaphors can actually be an improvement, say, talking about a hotel's refurbishment as a "face over"—a mix between a "face-lift" and a "makeover." I think that works better than either of the two original phrases!

BARE NECESSITIES
An overview of topless etiquette.

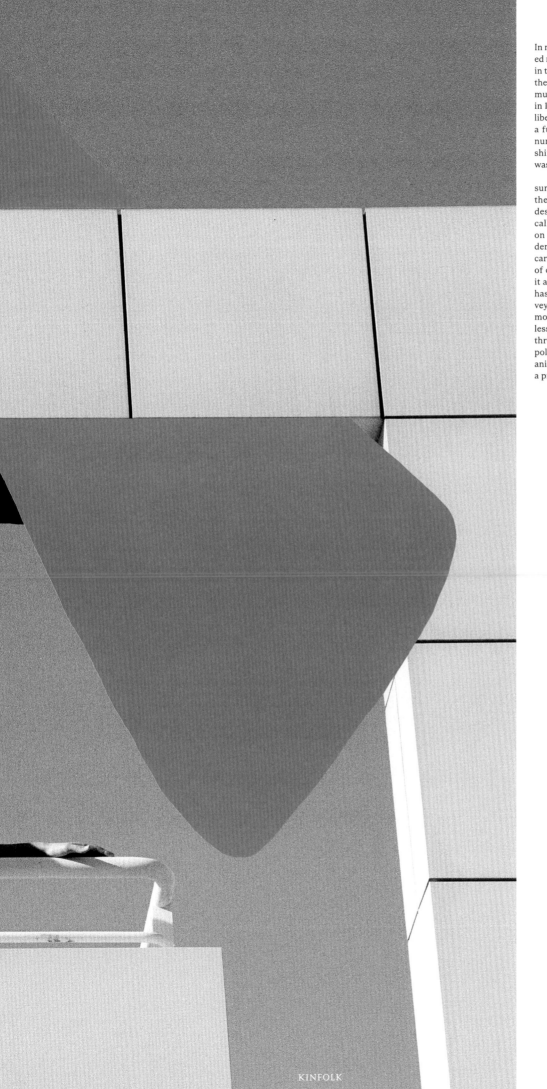

In modern times, the legality of sunbathing bare-breasted might seem like a question for women only. But back in the 1930s, it was American men campaigning to "free the nipple" after the shirtless success of Johnny Weissmuller in 1932's *Tarzan the Ape Man*, and Clark Gable in 1934's *It Happened One Night* awakened them to the liberating possibility of wearing something other than a full swimming costume to the beach. Only after a number of protests (42 men who swam together *sans* shirt in Atlantic City were arrested and fined in 1935) was "bareback bathing" finally legalized in 1937.

For women, the debate is not yet settled. Topless sunbathing's glamorous reputation was born during the sexual revolution of the 1960s. In 1964, fashion designer Rudi Gernreich created a topless swimsuit called the "monokini"—a high-waisted bikini brief on the bottom, and two thin, suspender-like shoulder straps on top. The French Riviera's reputation for carefree hedonism was built in large part on the image of celebrities—Brigitte Bardot among them—letting it all hang out in the sun. But nowadays, it seems one has to go elsewhere to get even tan lines: A 2019 survey found Spanish and German women are currently more open to the idea than the French. Despite topless sunbathing being legal in France, in August 2020, three beach-going women were asked to cover up by police. The country's interior minister, Gérald Darmanin, backed their right to bare, tweeting: "Freedom is a precious commodity."

WORDS
BELLA GLADMAN
PHOTO
AMANDA CHARCHIAN

KATIE PATERSON

WORDS
TOM FABER
PHOTOS
JAMES BENNETT

The artist making work for other planets.

Katie Paterson's garage contains moon dust. It's stored alongside offcuts from a mammoth's thighbone and a collection of wood samples from 10,000 different trees, each acquired in the name of art. In her work, Paterson poses searching existential questions in the form of poetic acts, whether that be setting up a live phone line to a melting glacier, sending a meteorite back into space or bouncing a recording of Beethoven's *Moonlight Sonata* off the surface of the moon. These artworks bring the cosmos down to scale, cutting through the detritus of daily life to reawaken a wide-eyed wonder at the universe and our place within it.

Paterson's work has been exhibited at London's Tate Britain, New York's Guggenheim Museum and the Scottish National Gallery of Modern Art. Her best-known project, *Future Library*, invites writers to submit original work that will remain unread until the year 2114, when a forest planted in 2014 in Norway will be fully grown to supply paper for the texts. So far she has solicited manuscripts from Margaret Atwood, Karl Ove Knausgård and Ocean Vuong. Paterson lives in a village outside Edinburgh, Scotland, with her partner and son.

TOM FABER: You don't come from a scientific background, yet much of your work revolves around astrophysics and geology. Where did this interest come from?

KATIE PATERSON: It crept up on me later in life. After my first degree at art school, I took off to live in Iceland for eight months. I worked at a hotel in a remote hamlet with just a fish factory, a petrol station, and nothing for miles around. It was summer, so there were 24 hours of daylight, and I started to tune into the wider sky, the wider universe. For the first time I saw the moon properly. It was life-changing. A lot of my artwork has come from that short moment in time.

TF: How did you start working with scientists?

KP: When I was at university I was trying to make art from Icelandic glacier ice and I wandered into the physics lab where they let me use their walk-in freezers. At first I was terrified of how they would perceive me, some straggly arts student coming in with a mad experiment, but actually they were always really welcoming.

TF: Scientists often put a lot of time and experimentation into your work. What do you think they get out of the collaboration?

KP: We give them an opportunity to bring to life some of their research, to show it in a museum and give it a wider audience. Often I'll ask a crazy question, like whether the European Space Agency can send a meteorite back into space, and they say: "Sure, why not?" This "why not" has kept me going. I think in the sciences there's less apprehension of risk. In the arts, we have so many deadlines and specifications, but in astrophysics, they're studying the edges of known space and time. It's not such a big deal when somebody comes along asking for something unexpected.

TF: Your work has included burying a grain of sand in the Sahara desert and writing condolence letters for dead stars.[1] Is the artwork the action itself, or is it communicating that action to an audience?

KP: It's both. The artworks are like musical scores—they place something in front of the audience, who take it and translate it into something new. If they're seeking to find out what the meaning is, that's great. But if they're just puzzled, or it's given them a laugh, that's fine, too.

TF: Often people expect contemporary art to be overly intellectual, or something you need to "get."

KP: Exactly; that's the problem. I don't want people to feel they

KP: I have a very bad sense of day-to-day time, which makes sense because my work shoots across billions of years. I'm always trying to reconcile with the 24-hour clock, to live with different ideas of time. And now I have a toddler so we have our everyday rituals and routines on top of that.

TF: Has having a child affected how you make art?

KP: Yeah, it's been an immense journey. He's three now, and it's incredible how he responds to things with such immediacy, seeing things almost magically. I particularly love reading children's stories to him because they use words as straightforwardly as possible. It's like what I try to achieve in my work, to avoid being convoluted but still have layers. I feel that if I can communicate an artwork easily to children, I've done quite well. Having a son has also tuned me into time in a different way. My *Future Library* project, where writers submit texts which won't be read for a hundred years, always confronts me with my own mortality.[2] But before I was just thinking about my lifetime, and now it's my son's. He might be alive to read those texts, even though I'll be gone.

TF: Is that sad to think about?

KP: It is. I used to take thinking about my death more lightly, but now I think about my son growing up, particularly the age he'll be when the *Future Library* is over, probably retired and in his 90s. But considering the environmental crisis now, it's important to underline that generational interaction. We need to take the focus off of our generation and start considering the generations to come.

TF: What do you think the world will look like in 2114, when the *Future Library* project ends?

KP: My deep down hope is that the forest itself is almost unchanged. But there's the alternative version where it's burned down, or there are insect infestations, or the land becomes flooded. We have to confront these apocalyptic visions in order to stop them from happening. My hope is that when the first reader opens the first page, they'll be looking back a hundred years and say: Thank goodness, they really took heed and made the changes that needed to happen.

TF: Do you think your art is hopeful?

KP: I think so. My artwork is looking at such big expanses of time, from a hundred years to a billion. It's trying to situate the human in a wider perspective, amongst other species, to allow us to jump outside of ourselves. Hopefully, it opens us up to the interconnectedness of things.

have to have a background in art history. The best artworks take you somewhere beyond, where there are no answers. In fact, they leave you with a kind of mystery, something you reach for with your intuition rather than your brain.

TF: One of your pieces was a black firework fired into the night sky at an undisclosed location. Another was a note of classical music being beamed under the ocean. These might be observed by nobody. What is art if there's nobody to witness it?

KP: It's almost like a Zen koan [riddle] approach to art. Ultimately, that's what artists do. They put something out there and hope it will have a repercussion.

TF: A lot of your work involves music. How does this overlap with your astronomical interests?

KP: I grew up in a house with a big vinyl collection so there was always music on, and my dad is a musician. Music can shift your atmosphere, taking you to places beyond words. When I beamed a composition to the moon, the signal was reflected back to earth with gaps in it, and that was played by a piano in a gallery. I chose *Moonlight Sonata* because I wanted to send a song written about the moon, but also because it's so familiar that people would instantly identify those gaps in the score— the moon's alterations.

TF: Your work also delves into a sense of deep, geological time. Do these concerns change how you view your own life?

(1)   In her ongoing project *The Dying Star Letters*, Paterson receives notifications from astronomical institutes each time a star explodes and writes a condolence letter to mark its passing. She issues between three and 150 such letters every week.

(2)   Ocean Vuong told *The Guardian* that he wanted to participate because "so much of publishing is about seeing your name in the world, but this is the opposite, putting the future ghost of you forward."

The technique Paterson is using in the image above is called *suminagashi*, a Japanese marbling technique that translates as "ink floating."

Part 2.
FEATURES
Fan Bingbing, fandoms and new fashion.
50 — 112

50	Fan Bingbing
60	Fractured Frequencies
70	At Work With: Maniera Gallery
78	Lido Pimienta
90	Home Tour: Lucinda Chambers
98	Fan the Flames
102	Kevin Abstract

Words
LAVENDER AU

TE WOMAN WHO CHANGED TE FACE OF CHINA.

FAN
Bingbing

I saw Fan Bingbing many times in Beijing—staring at me from inside elevators, metro stations, airports and malls—before I ever saw one of her movies. She made her name as an actress, but ask anyone and they will tell you that pigeonholing her is to misunderstand who she is. In 2018, she crashed the server of a popular e-commerce platform by posting about a facial mask she liked.

Fan, who was born in 1981, started her career 20 years before "influencer" became a common term, but that is the only word that encapsulates what she is. No one looked like her before, but now, everyone does. Her eggshell-pale skin, large eyes and diamond-shaped jawline have inspired thousands of knockoffs. I have a hypothesis that the default filter on Meitu—China's photoshop app of choice—makes everyone look like her. Fan is more than her looks, though, she's a business.

Due to COVID, I speak to Fan on a WeChat video call. She's in a photography studio in Beijing, and has just wrapped up a shoot. It doesn't seem much warmer than outside: Her hair is hidden in a black beanie, and she's wearing an egg-shaped down jacket with chunky braids down its front from local designer Christopher Bu. Her face fills my phone screen, her skin so white it glows. After seeing umpteen imitations, coming face to face with the original is disconcerting.

Like everyone else, Fan has been affected by the pandemic, which stalled the production and release of films in China. She has found new ways to fill the time. She's tried her hand at cooking—in her case, poké bowls. And part of her daily routine is to stay up until 2 or 3 a.m., watching beauty tutorials or videos on Douyin (the original TikTok), and scrolling Instagram for inspiration. She admits that going to sleep late is a bad habit of hers, and it seems she won't be breaking it any time soon: "Time passes so quickly, I'm reluctant to sleep."

Fan is making up for lost time. Just when she was poised to have it all, in 2018, she went through a brutal reversal of fortune. It started with a grudge borne by a former talk show host, Cui Yongyuan. Fan had acted in popular director Feng Xiaogang's movie *Cell Phone*, which bore a striking resemblance to Cui's personal life. He had complained publicly about being hounded by journalists when the film was released—the lead character has an affair and finds himself replaced at work by his mistress—and Fan was about to act in its sequel. He first

(above)
Fan wears a dress by MIU MIU and a
ring by MAISON SANS TITRE.

claimed she was paid around $1.5 million for four days' work, supposedly on *Cell Phone II*. He then leaked another document, as proof she used a dual-contract to avoid paying taxes. The second contract listed that she was actually paid closer to $8 million. The news blew up on social media. Fan's team denied

the allegations. Then, she disappeared.

Once an image of aspiration, Fan became a target for public resentment. The Chinese release of *Air Strike* was canceled. The release of *L.O.R.D.: Legend of Ravaging Dynasties 2*, a fantasy adventure film in which she had a leading role, was postponed. And it was rumored that the team behind the historical drama *Legend of Ba Qing* was transposing another actress's face over hers. The fallout also affected her brother, a singer and actor, and her then-fiancé, the actor Li Chen. They both found their work frozen.

Other stars frantically filed their taxes to avoid Fan's fate. A new rule was put in place, likely inspired by the astronomical amounts listed on her contracts: Actors' pay was capped at 40% of production costs and lead actors limited to 70% of total pay for actors.

The media began to censor coverage of Fan. Her social media went quiet. Her admirers asked where she was. Her younger brother wept in a meeting with his fans, and said somewhat ominously, "I don't know if I'll still be standing here 10 years later." Her wedding never took place. Pictures of the pink-themed birthday party where Li proposed had lit up social media the year before; as had his engagement gift—an Enchanted Doll customized by designer Marina Bychkova to look like her. Fan was placed under house arrest. Three months of silence later, a public letter appeared on her Weibo account, in which she apologized to her fans and the nation.

When I ask Fan about the tax evasion incident, she gives me almost exactly the same answer she gave *The New York Times* just over a year ago—"No one's life will always be smooth sailing." She adds that she's always been the kind of person willing to face difficulties.

Fan has been working hard since she was a child. In fact, Fan says that because she didn't have much time to play with dolls

Styling
EVAN FENG

(above)   Fan wears a dress by MONCLER X JW ANDERSON and a shirt and hat by THOM BROWNE.
(right)   She wears a dress by VALENTINO and jewelry by MAISON SANS TITRE.

" To feel no shame inside, THAT'S what's most important."

when she was younger, she still does it now, describing it as relaxing. Her collection includes rare Barbies and Japanese ball-jointed dolls.

She grew up in east China in the port city of Yantai. Her father sang in the naval force's art troupe and her mother was a dancer. After attending television and film school in Shanghai, she appeared on television in 1998, as a maid in a *My Fair Princess*, a popular palace drama—think *Twelfth Night* set in the Qing dynasty.

But it was the part of a television host's mistress in *Cell Phone*—the highest grossing film of 2003—that made her a household name. By then, she was represented by the agency owned by film conglomerate Huayi Brothers. Four years later, in 2007, she started Fan Bingbing Studio. There, she invested, produced and acted in her own films, and started a celebrity-making machine of her own. By the time she starred in *Lost in Thailand* in 2012, which became the first movie in China to earn over one billion yuan ($150 million), Fan was enough of a celebrity that she simply played herself.

She'd already built a public persona as the epitome of the modern power woman and gained the nickname "Master Fan" —even though in Chinese, "master" is usually reserved for men. When asked by a reporter whether she'd marry into a rich family, Fan replied, "I am rich." It became her defining quote. She proved deft at pithy comebacks. To a common criticism of her, which compared her to a vase (beautiful outside, empty inside), she retorted, "If I am one, it's a precious one, which can't be put just anywhere."

The fact that Fan always plays strong female roles is part of her attraction. She has tapped into a consciousness that many women identify with, and look up to. She's a consort who ascends the ranks of the Tang dynasty court to become the empire's only female ruler. She's a masseuse in Beijing, taking her child and running away from the two men who want to control her life. She's an animation who wields mystical powers. Many of her fans are from the post-Cultural Revolution generations, educated and cherished only daughters. They want it all—in their personal lives and careers. Fan, in their eyes, is a success story.

Her rise coincided with China's film industry boom and its expansion beyond theaters into home entertainment and merchandise. China's studios now rival those of Hollywood. Instead of Universal, Paramount, Disney and Warner, China has Huayi Brothers, Tencent Pictures and Huanxi Media, to name just a few. While Chinese audiences turn up for *The Avengers*, they also come out for homegrown patriotic blockbusters like *Wolf Warrior* and *The Eight Hundred*. For Hollywood movies, hiring a Chinese star is a way to improve their chances of being included in the quota, set by the film regulator, for foreign films let into China—and ultimately ensuring a sizeable audience. This may be the reason for Fan's casting as Blink in *X-Men: Days of Future Past*, in which she has one line.

Perhaps more than in other countries, China's celebrities must set a moral example. Fan's family are Communist Party members, which is common for people of her stature, although stars in China tend to stay out of the nuts and bolts of politics unless it's to spread what the government terms "positive energy" in the form of patriotic movies. Fan has played her part as a People's Liberation Army fighter pilot in *Sky Hunter*. She has also turned her red carpet appearances into a show of patriotism, representing Chinese film abroad. Before the tax scandal, Fan frequently showed up

(right)   Fan wears a dress by VALENTINO and a necklace by MAISON SANS TITRE.

FEATURES

on best-dressed lists for her appearances at international film circuits—sometimes the only Chinese actress to get a mention. Her parade down the red carpet at the 2010 Cannes Film Festival, in an imperial yellow gown with dragons flying up from its hem, is part of the country's collective memory.

Just under a year after the scandal, in 2019, Fan reentered the public eye at an anniversary gala for streaming company iQIYI. Her understated Alexander McQueen trouser suit and De Beers diamonds were a far cry from her red carpet gowns. She arrived with little fanfare, long after most guests had arrived, and didn't take questions from the media. At the gala's private dinner, she made toasts and played party games. It seemed she was testing the waters, to see if she'd be accepted once more. When photos circulated on Weibo, the reaction was sometimes vitriolic—some users thought she should be banned from acting for life. She accepts this criticism as part of her job: "The most important thing is whether or not what you're doing now is right or not, isn't it?" she says. "To feel no shame inside, that's what's most important."

Fan has a small circle of close friends, who she says stood by her through the scandal. "They made me feel the world was still warm," she says. On her birthday last year, when she turned 39, she wrote a post in which she appeared to thank the 15 people in the industry who still wished her a happy birthday. She seems sanguine about this loss of fair-weather friends. "I knew at a very young age that not everyone would be your friend," she says. "There are only three to five people you can call true friends."

For the last few years, during which Fan hasn't appeared on the silver screen, there's no sign she's given up on a comeback.[1] "I've never really thought about what life after retirement would be like," she says. Instead, she's pivoted, or perhaps "leaned in" to what she'd always been—herself.

Recently, Fan has become a star of the phone screen. In livestreams and short videos, she applies skincare masks and pats serums onto her face. The public have welcomed her back on social-shopping app Xiaohongshu, where she had already started building a following prior to the scandal. Its motto is "find the life you want," and more than 300 million users share reviews of lifestyle products. Fan now has a following of 12 million on the app, where she posts—among other tips—her pre-flight routine which includes her own 15-minute facial massage technique. She began by advertising products from other brands, but has since started her own line—Fan Beauty. Soon after her appearance at the iQIYI gala, she launched a sea grape face mask. This way of connecting with the public is better for Fan at the moment: it doesn't rely on industry intermediaries, many of whom are still nervous about being associated with her.

Fan will return to movie screens in *The 355*, which is due for release next year. Cast before the scandal, Fan joins Jessica Chastain, Penélope Cruz, Lupita Nyong'o and Diane Kruger in a Hollywood spy sisterhood film, where they hunt down a weapon that could destroy the world. She says she learned a lot from filming *The 355*, specifically, how her co-stars manage their work-life balance. "Because I spend most of my time working, I have less time to see friends, less time for my pets, less time to spend with family," she says.

"I pass on hope," Fan says simply, when I ask her what role she plays in her family. Fan's younger brother, Fan Chengcheng, has

Hair Stylist
GAO JIAN
Makeup Artist
HU YIYIN

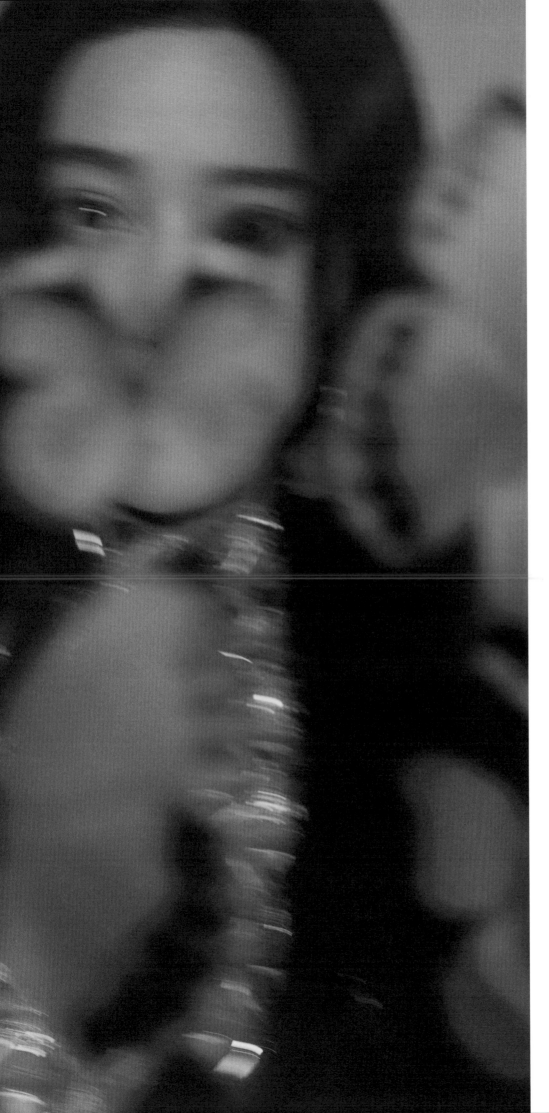

followed her into the entertainment industry. He joined the aptly named reality television show *Idol Producer* where, inspired by South Korean celebrity boot camps, male trainees compete to be part of a nine-member pop group—he made it in.

He is 19 years her junior, and when I ask her what's changed between when she joined the industry and when he did, she says, "It's so different." This is the most forceful statement Fan has given since we started speaking. She proceeds to explain how superstars lived on, in the memories of her generation. "They would be remembered for a long time, respected for a long time," she says. Now, it's not the same. "Maybe someone likes a star one day, and then the next day, someone similar comes along." In the current entertainment scene, she says there's always someone else who can play the same role—it's rare to have parts where only one person will do.

Perhaps it's the machine, perhaps it's the audience. In any case, Fan thinks the celebrity assembly line doesn't create many legends any more. Being an icon—being her—is a rarity. Maybe the reason young actors can't make a lasting impression is because so many of them are trying to be Fan Bingbing.

(1) In May 2020, it was announced that Fan would return to television screens via the Chinese video service Youku. She stars in *Win the World*, a period drama set in the Qin dynasty, and plays the role of a widowed entrepreneur who helps bankroll the construction of the Great Wall of China. *South China Morning Post* reported that, with a budget of $70 million, the series is the most expensive in China's history.

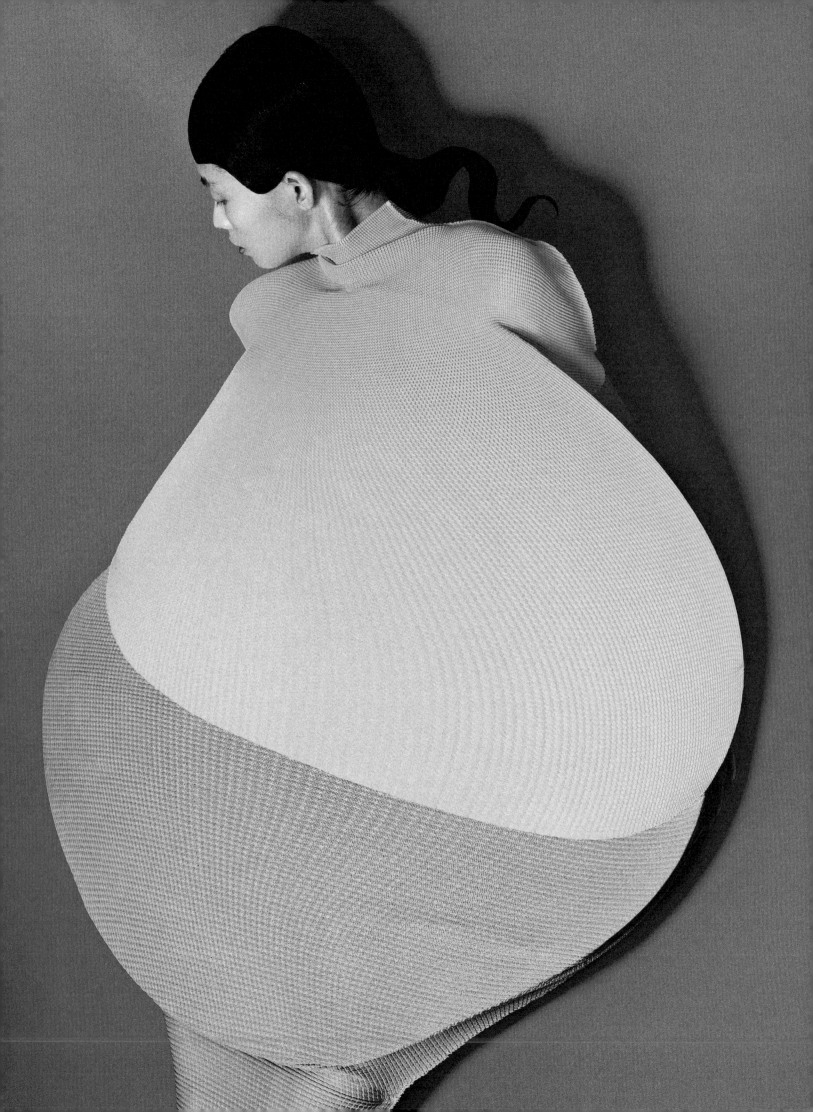

Summer style
catches a strange
new wave.

61   FRACTURED
            FREQUENCIES

Photography
ZHONGLIN
Styling
CHEN YU

(previous)   Chen wears two turtlenecks by ME ISSEY MIYAKE.
(below   She wears a bodysuit, boots and a fishnet paper dress by JISOO JANG.
& right)

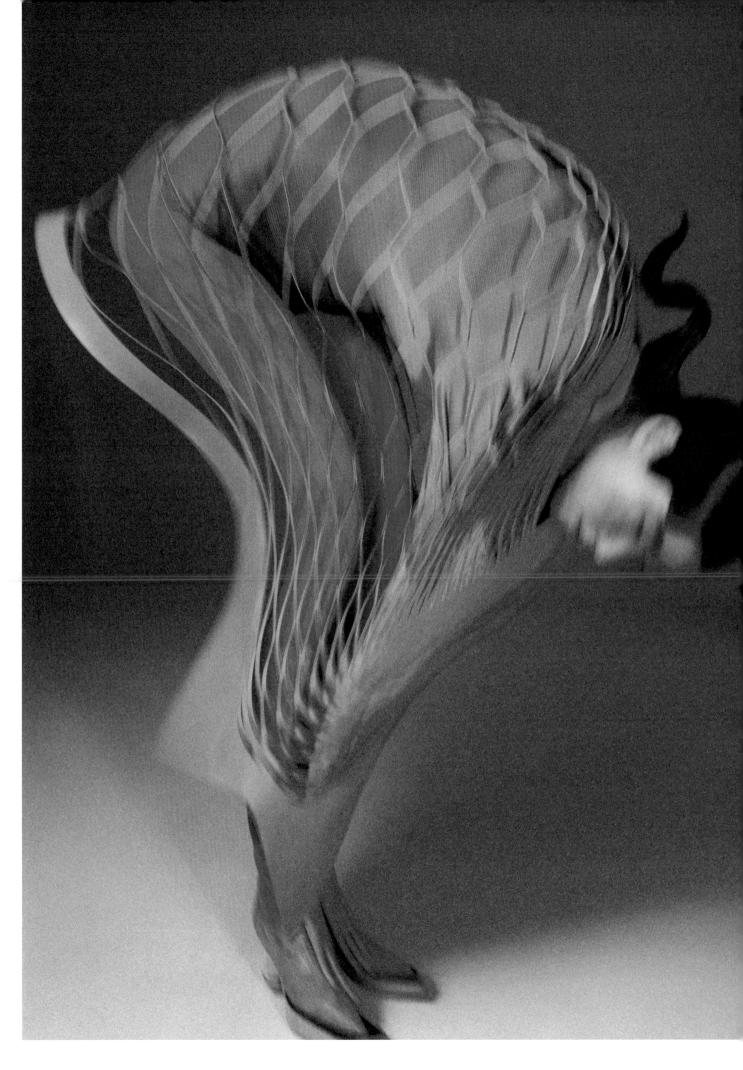

(all)   Chen wears a headdress, jacket, top, vest and skirt by ROBERT WUN.

(above) Chen wears a printed top by ME ISSEY MIKAYE over another top and skirt by PLEATS PLEASE ISSEY MIYAKE.
(right) She wears knitwear by JISOO JANG.

(left)   Chen wears a scarf and trousers by BOTTEGA VENETA.
(below)   She wears a dress by BOTTEGA VENETA and a fishnet paper dress by JISOO JANG.

Hair Stylist
WEIC LIN
Makeup Artist
FIONA LI
Model
CHEN HSU

AT WORK WITH:
Maniera Gallery

Words by
Anna Winston

"It is, how do you call it... *a graveyard*. Everything that went wrong ends up here."

As graveyards go, the home of Amaryllis Jacobs and Kwinten Lavigne is surprisingly high up and sun-filled. Their apartment—also home to their daughter and two cats—is far from the pristine, high-design showroom that might be expected of the founders of Maniera, the Brussels gallery that has forged an unusual and much-admired path through the collectible design market over the last seven years.

Since launching in 2014, Maniera has distinguished itself by commissioning new furniture and homeware from individuals or practices who have never made this type of object before—initially architects, but also artists and other designers in recent years. Bijoy Jain, Anne Holtrop and Bernard Dubois number among the long list of people that Jacobs and Lavigne have cajoled into making something new and unusual for the gallery.

A five-minute bike ride from the city-center gallery, the couple's home is dotted with prototypes from these collaborations. It is a stylish final resting place for rather attractive corpses. Maniera pieces—even those that remained prototypes and didn't exhibit—would be treated as precious objects elsewhere. "It's very eclectic," says Jacobs, smiling, still in her brightly printed dressing gown. "We are less keen on our interior than most of our clients, that's for sure," says Lavigne, a stark contrast to his partner, in a severe turtleneck.

Under normal circumstances, Jacobs and Lavigne are frequently on the move, traveling to see the architects and artists they commission, to meet makers who can realize their designs, or to attend art and design fairs in places like Milan, Basel and St. Moritz. "We are not often here," explains Jacobs. The pandemic has kept them in one place but it hasn't slowed them down. With everyone at home more and spending less on day-to-day conveniences, there is more interest in the remarkable interior objects that Maniera creates. "*Touchons du bois*, knock on wood, so far it's been quite okay," says Jacobs.

The couple have an easy, infectious energy. Rather than completing each other's sentences, they develop each other's thoughts, sometimes adding a gentle jibe;

"She doesn't listen," pouts Lavigne and Jacobs laughs. They first met 15 years ago when Jacobs was at BOZAR, the Centre for Fine Arts in Brussels, where she led the education department. One of her projects involved Arts Basics for Children (ABC), the organization where Lavigne worked.

In the late 2000s, architecture from Flanders, the northern region of Belgium, was the hot ticket. "At the Venice Architecture Biennale, all the best projects were Flemish projects," Jacobs recalls. Her original plan was to start a PR agency for these up-and-coming architects, but they couldn't afford her. The solution was to commission them instead. Lavigne was by then working as head of production at WIELS, the center for contemporary art in Brussels. Maniera was born as a combination of their expertise and interests.

"We have had to find a way to work and live together harmoniously," says Jacobs. "We each do something different. I am most of the time in the gallery, and Kwinten is most of the time on the road or in the workshop." Choosing who to commission next is a joint decision, she says. Lavigne agrees, but adds a caveat: "Amaryllis is more on this social media of Instagram and so on, and this way she has a better view of what is happening," he says. "So of course, she is proposing [collaborators] more than me."

While most galleries want to showcase artists or designers performing at the top of their respective fields, Maniera encourages its exhibitors to try something they have never done before. "It became clear for us that it was just interesting to ask people to do something next to their profession," explains Lavigne, "to take them out of their comfort zone." Do they ever struggle? "All of [the architects] go through a crisis," says Jacobs, and they both laugh. The Maniera brief forces collaborators to interrogate their creative identity and then work out how to translate it into a piece of furniture. The result is always surprising.[1]

Although it feels fresh in Maniera's hands, this crossing of disciplines is not new. Sixty years ago, it wasn't unusual for an architect to design a building and everything that went in it, down to the door handles. Many of the most enduring 20th-century design classics are by architects: Alvar Aalto's

Photography by Martina Bjorn

(1)   Bijoy Jain's work for Maniera Gallery includes a series of seats in which the backrest is made out of tiny bricks, stacked like a wall.
(2)   The Collectible fair doesn't showcase vintage design classics. Instead, it shows the work of contemporary creatives; a market that has been booming for
          decades when it comes to art, but is relatively underdeveloped within the design world.

Paimio Chair, Frank Gehry's bentwood furniture collection, Poul Henningsen's Artichoke Lamp. Nostalgia for this total design control, combined with the pace of furniture design—invigoratingly fast, compared to building projects that take years to complete—has made the Maniera proposition particularly appealing to architects.

The couple's enthusiasm and open brief makes them charmingly persuasive. Almost everyone they have asked has signed on instantly, including an increasing number of non-architects like the Swiss textile designer Christoph Hefti, a longtime Dries Van Noten collaborator revered within the fashion industry. For Maniera, he creates richly textural wall hangings and rugs, reinterpreting folkloric images and symbols into a distinctive, almost hallucinatory visual style. Upcoming projects include collections with two of Japan's most vaunted architects, Kazuyo Sejima of Sanaa and Junya Ishigami.

"The most important thing is the freedom we offer them," explains Jacobs. "Not telling them, 'This is not ergonomic, this is not sellable,'... Sometimes you think, 'This is

impossible, we will never make it, it is too difficult or too expensive,' but somehow we have always managed."

Lavigne often plays the diplomat, convincing skeptical Belgian manufacturers to take on complicated, small-run, inefficient projects, and managing the different styles of each collaborator. Some, like the Amsterdam-based architect Anne Holtrop, need to make things themselves as part of their process, while Bijoy Jain of Studio Mumbai has cultivated a world of skilled craftspeople in and around his studio.

In recent years, Belgium—a cultural hub in the 16th and 17th centuries—has gone through a design renaissance. Since 2018, it has been home to Collectible, the world's first dedicated collectible design fair.[2] There are galleries all over the city and growing numbers of young design graduates are taking over spaces around its peripheries or a short train ride away. The region around Brussels is rich with private collectors. And the city benefits from being the mid-point in the railway artery that connects London, Paris and Amsterdam.

Despite their international roster, Maniera's founders believe the gallery could not have succeeded anywhere other than Brussels—even though, says Lavigne, Belgians have a habit of undervaluing their own: "You always have to prove yourself abroad first." In the beginning, it was the American market, driven by interior designers curating homes for wealthy clients, that bought from and supported Maniera. "Brussels at that time was very sexy, it was the new Berlin... It seemed everything that happened in Brussels ended up in *The New York Times*," recalls Jacobs.

Maniera helped establish this Belgian scene. It has earned credibility in doing so, and this has given its founders the freedom to work with younger creatives—like 25-year-old designer Lukas Gschwandtner, whose first pieces debuted at Maniera in a performative sculptural installation in February 2021. The next dream is to have a depot, a home for their archive. "We have every first piece from every collection. It's our little treasure, the archive," Jacobs says. "It's so sad that it's all wrapped up."

FEATURES

John White Alexander, ... Oil on Canvas
William Dargie, Yellow ... Oil on Canvas
Nikolai Bodarevsky, ... 1850–1921, Oil on Canvas

← POLICE - POLITIE

Photography
TED BELTON

Words
DAPHNÉE DENIS

LIDO

THE ALTERNATIVE MISS COLOMBIA

IS SEIZING HER CROWN.

It was awkward. Cringe-inducing. Meme-worthy. And a mistake. But above all, for many Colombians, Steve Harvey erroneously crowning and then de-crowning their country's beauty queen during the 2015 Miss Universe contest quite simply amounted to a declaration of war.[1] The TV mishap, whereby Colombia (well, Miss Colombia) lost a beauty title it never really earned to the Philippines (well, Miss Philippines), sent shockwaves through the South American nation, unveiling the dark underbelly of misguided pageant nationalism. For weeks, overtly racist comments about Harvey, who is African American, and Pia Alonzo Wurtzbach, the Filipino Miss Universe, were commonplace. For producer-singer-songwriter Lido Pimienta, the debacle was a wake-up call. Though she had left her native Barranquilla for Canada years prior, being abroad didn't shelter her from hearing hurtful comments: As a queer Afro-Indigenous woman, she says, Miss Colombia-gate made her question how she fit in her home country, if at all.

"People would say: 'Of course, it had to be that Black man,' or 'Why would the crown go to that Chinese lady?'," Pimienta recalls of the commentary surrounding Miss Universe. "I'd been trying to find my place in Canada for five years, and when this happened, I wondered: 'Did I ever have my place in Colombia?' I realized I'm not from here or there. And I'm actually a lot from there, but people who are a lot from there don't belong in the mainstream."

This is true: In some ways, one cannot get more Colombian than Pimienta. On her mother's side, she descends from the Wayuu people, the largest Indigenous ethnic group in the country. Her father, whom she credits with passing his love of music on to her, was Black. This heritage isn't unusual, but as she rightly points out, Native and Afro-Colombian people continue to be overlooked, even demeaned, in a country that hasn't yet fully reckoned with its colonial past. White descendants of the Spanish, *criollos*, hold power and dictate beauty standards. "When the media portrays Colombia as a place where everyone looks like [actor] Sofia Vergara, it's wrong, you know?" Pimienta says. From this realization, her latest album emerged: the critically acclaimed *Miss Colombia*, which she describes as a "cynical love letter" to her home, a breakup symphony of sorts.

Today, the 34-year-old is self-quarantining in Toronto after a work trip to Mexico.[2] She's taking my questions over Zoom while eating granola, her cat sporadically popping up on screen. As we speak, *Miss Colombia*—which Pimienta hasn't been able to tour with due to the pandemic—is nominated for a Grammy for Best Latin Rock or Alternative Album, an institutional nod to her uncompromising vision. Her music, a raw, emotional blend of her powerful voice, DIY electronic beats and traditional rhythms from Colombia's

(1)   Moments after being announced as Miss Universe in 2015, the crown was removed from Ariadna Gutiérrez Arévalo, Miss Colombia, and given instead to Pia Alonzo Wurtzbach, Miss Philippines.
(2)   Pimienta brought her own clothes to this photo shoot and chose to wear many of the outfits that she had brought back from her trip to Mexico.

Caribbean coast, defies expectations of what contemporary "Latin" music should sound like to achieve global reach. Her previous record, *La Papessa*, which was written in Spanish, earned her Canada's prestigious Polaris Prize, making her the first artist to receive the award for an album sung in a language other than English or French. Upon accepting the honor, which effectively meant Canada claiming her as one of its own, she quipped: "Perhaps the only thing that I can say is that I hope that the Aryan specimen who told me to go back to my country two weeks after arriving in London, Ontario, Canada, is watching this." She then thanked the country's Indigenous tribes, the "protectors of the land," for allowing her to be their guest.

Activism has always been part of Pimienta's art. Much of her musical awakening came with the awareness of what it meant to be a person of color in a country that takes her intersecting cultures for granted. Though she used to sing in a metal band and likens her teenage years to the notorious Larry Clark film *Kids* (minus the sex), Caribbean music and traditions imbued her upbringing too. Her "formal" training as a singer, she says, came from street performers from San Basilio de Palenque, the first free enclave of the Americas, founded by formerly enslaved people.[3] The town remains steeped in poverty despite Colombia owing its people the Afro-inspired rhythms of *mapalé*, *champeta* and *cumbia*.

" Nobody told me what to do but I made the right decisions."

Pimienta would join the musicians of Palenque's legendary Afro-Caribbean group Sexteto Tabalá during the Barranquilla Carnival, witnessing firsthand the lack of institutional support for the musicians' artistry. "Only during Carnival, or when some politician wants to pretend they care about Black people, are these groups from Palenque called out to perform," she says, switching from Spanish into English. "And then, they go back in the closet." A testament to her roots, *Miss Colombia* features Sexteto Tabalá on one of its tracks.[4] The town's traditional dance collective Kumbé is the flamboyant main act of the video she directed to accompany the song "Eso Que Tu Haces." One of the verses sums up her feelings for a country that won't love her back: "That thing you do," she laments, "it isn't love."

Pimienta started working on her own music soon after moving to Canada at the age of 18, drawing inspiration from traditional Caribbean sounds, trip hop and early reggaeton beats by the likes

(3)   Known as Palenquero, or *lengua* ("tongue"), the language spoken in San Basilio de Palenque is thought to be the only Spanish-based Creole language in Latin America.

(4)   Sexteto Tabalá mixes Caribbean musical styles, like *bullerengue* and *porro*, with *lumbalú*, the Bantu funeral chants of San Basilio de Palenque. The group appears on Pimienta's song "Quiero Que Me Salves."

of Tego Calderón (she eyerolls at the current success of the genre, dismissing it as whitewashed and uninteresting). She is quick to dismiss her first EP, *Color*, which was produced by an ex-partner, as "a little girl's fantasy who put her music in the hands of someone bad." Still, Pimienta says it made her realize she needed to teach herself record production so no one would claim ownership of her art again.

She learned the craft via YouTube tutorials and collaborations with Myspace-bred electro artists like Argentina's Chancha Via Circuito, recording *La Papessa* in her laundry room with a sheet over her head to mute any reverberating sounds. That record, which would put her on the map of Canada's alternative scene, turned the pain of a romantic breakup into self-empowerment.[5] "I wasn't born to fit in a heteronormative telenovela," she sings in "La Capacidad." "I wasn't born to hold back feminism worldwide." On tour, she makes a point of asking women of color, transgender women, and women with disabilities to come to the front of the audience.

As far as Pimienta is concerned, however, *Miss Colombia* is her first album, meaning the first project she created on purpose, trusting her own voice. "When I made it, I was very aware of the power of my words, of my music," she says. "I love that nobody wrote my songs, nobody told me what to do but I made the right decisions. It gave me self-validation." The album's cover presents her satirical take on the beauty queen ideal, portraying her as a colorful if nostalgic *quinceañera* virgin-bride about to get baptized—a sum of the tropes surrounding the impossibly ideal Colombian woman. Reclaiming herself as the opposite of that cliché made her grow, she adds: "I realized, Wow, I am amazing." Leaving Colombia behind, no longer romanticizing it, may just have been worth it.

(5)   *La Papessa* translates from Spanish as "The High Priestess," a card commonly used in tarot. "It means to me what the card means to a lot of people," Pimienta told CBC when the album won a Polaris Prize in 2017. "To concentrate and focus and have knowledge... and not let anything distract you from your goals."

Hair & Makeup
RAHNELL BRANTON
Set Design
CAITLIN DOHERTY

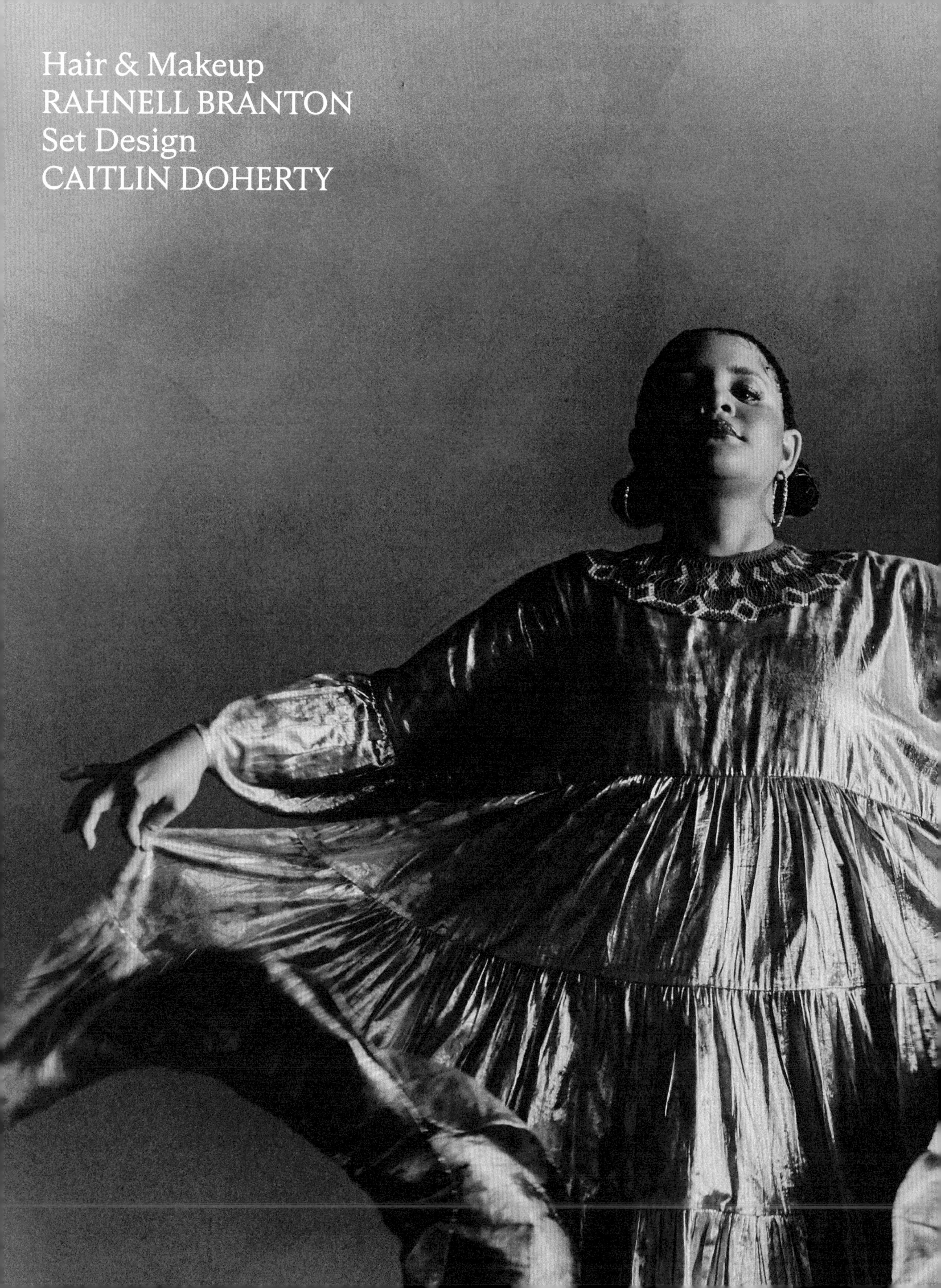

HOME TOUR:
Lucinda Chambers

Words
GEORGE UPTON

Inside the west London townhouse at the heart of the British fashion establishment.

Visiting Lucinda Chambers at home feels like being taken into her confidence. The interior of her handsome Edwardian house in west London, where she has lived for more than 30 years, has evolved slowly. Here, in the layers of color and pattern, textiles and photographs, is the same eclectic, impulsive style with which Chambers made her name as the fashion director of *British Vogue*. It's also where, after she was let go from *Vogue* in 2017 and thought her career was over, she began to combine her work as a stylist with her new role as a designer. She is now the co-founder of an e-commerce platform, Collagerie, and the fashion label Colville.

There is something intimate about being surrounded by the accumulation of a lifetime's worth of decisions: a wall of plates above the bath, a grid of framed vintage wallpaper samples, an array of colorful paper lampshades hanging in the stairwell. Chambers shares the house with her husband, Simon Crow, but she has always had free rein over its decoration—even when the couple's three sons were living at home. Take the staircase, for example, which for many years had been painted bright pink, until one day she came back from a shoot abroad and saw it with new eyes. "It was like walking into a mad old lady's house," Chambers recalls. "The carpet on the stairs was bright green, red and yellow. It was eye-watering. I realized I had to change it." Her solution is certainly more muted, though it is no less eccentric. "I really wanted to make it look like a German urinal, so I painted it half shiny brown and half gray, all the way up to the top."

Chambers has always gone her own way, a fact that was evident even in her first shoot for *British Vogue* in the mid-1980s. "I had been working as an assistant for years and eventually the editor, Beatrix Miller, gave me the chance to do my own shoot," she recalls. "I could choose anyone I liked

The hallway is painted the same "German urinal" combination of glossy brown and gray as the staircase.

to photograph it, so I rang up Patrick Demarchelier and went to New York. It was supposed to be a beauty story but I had the model wearing a towering stack of hats, and her legs going through the sleeves of a jumper that I had turned inside out." On the flight back she was certain that she was

going to be fired, but Miller liked it. Chambers soon became known for her distinctive and particularly creative approach to styling. At 25, she was made fashion director at *Elle* when it launched in the UK, and a few years later, when Alexandra Shulman was appointed editor-in-chief of *British Vogue* in 1992, she returned to the magazine to become fashion director, a position she held until Shulman was replaced by Edward Enninful in 2017.

On set, she has always worked like a sculptor, manipulating clothes with the economy of experience: adjusting the drapery of a long skirt, folding a sleeve back, untucking just the right amount of shirt. "Alex [Shulman] would always tell me to 'leave the bloody clothes alone,' but I never can," she says, laughing. "Something happens to me when I'm on a shoot. I just want the picture that I want to do, and I'm always madly optimistic that whoever commissioned it will love it."

Chambers is speaking to me from the room at the front of the house that is currently doubling as her office. There's a fire going, and she is surrounded by color and texture: the vibrant red of the walls, the striped cushions made up from fabric she's collected, the floral print sofa made by a friend, and the shaggy rug in red, white and brown that was produced by artisans in Turkey for Colville, the brand Chambers founded in 2018 with the designer Molly Molloy. The pair had worked together at Marni, where Chambers had been a long-standing creative consultant, "making the sort of clothes we wanted to wear." After Marni was sold and its direction changed, they started their own project with the same ethos.

(right)   The Turkish rug is part of the COLVILLE collection. Its design reflects the fiery tones that dominate Chambers' home.

" I grew up in houses where you could
put your feet up on the table. It's very different
to what people are doing now."

For the first two years, the focus was on clothes. Then came the pandemic, and, naturally, a homeware collection. Items from the collection sit happily among Chambers' other belongings; her Moroccan poof is now draped with a Colville blanket. There is something assured and perhaps innate in her aesthetic. "I don't take a long time to think about what I want to do," she explains.

The key to finding this easy balance, Chambers explains, is comfort. "It's a really underrated thing, both in clothes and at home," she says. Despite the ceramics and glassware clustered on shelves and mantelpieces, or the letters and drawings that cover the walls in the kitchen, this is not a place where—if you were to pick up something that caught your eye—you would disturb some intricately curated scheme. Mugs of tea are placed straight down on the table without a coaster. "I grew up in houses that you could really live in, where you could throw yourself on the sofa and put your feet up on the table," Chambers says. "It's very different to what people are doing now, growing up with Instagram, where everything is carefully designed and used as a photo opportunity."

Chambers moved often when she was younger. Her mother earned a living renovating houses and selling them on, and Chambers and her brother lived in a succession of work-in-progress properties in west London, though always within walking distance of Harrods and the Brompton Oratory. "We never moved off page 58 of the A to Z," she says. "That was ring-fenced for us." Chambers's mother had always had side jobs, making jam and sewing school

Chambers' west London home is referred to by some friends as The Crowtel (her husband's name being Crow) for its warm welcome.

uniforms, until she went to art school in her late 50s, became a bookbinder and went on to write 10 books for Thames and Hudson on marbling and decorative papers. It instilled in Chambers a hands-on, can-do attitude. "She was a great person for rolling up her sleeves and doing it herself," she says. "And I feel I am as well."

Chambers thinks that it is as a consequence of her peripatetic childhood that she has never wanted to move. Unlike her mother, who was always knocking down walls and relocating staircases, she has altered little of the fabric of the house. Yet the restless creativity that defined her youth is still evident. Walls have been

painted and repainted; furniture—sourced from Portobello Road Market and *brocantes* near her house in France—have been rotated through rooms; objects, collected "magpie-like" while on shoots around the world, are arranged on mantelpieces or hung from doorknobs.

"Whether it's for the body or for houses, it really all comes down to decoration," she says. "I think if something's really pleasurable on the eye, it lifts the spirits."

For her birthday a few years ago, Chambers bought herself the services of a professional picture hanger. Her collection of paintings and photography—Edward Weston, René Burri, Malick Sidibé, and past collaborators including Sheila Metzner and Mario Testino—form a patchwork up the walls of the unorthodox brown-gray stairs.[1] It's typical of Chambers—inventive and impulsive. Where her neighbors are regularly gutting their homes, adding basements and extensions, and selling them on, Chambers is content to largely let the house age as if it is a living thing, their relationship a kind of symbiosis. "It's a work in progress," she says, smiling. "We never do anything in one go, I enjoy tinkering with it too much."

(1) Chambers and the famed photographer Mario Testino began collaborating early on in their careers. Speaking to *The Telegraph* in 2012, Testino recalled how he first spotted Chambers' "shocking bleached blonde hair" from the top deck of a bus on Regent's Street. A short while later he was called in to photograph new cuts at a hair salon and she happened to be the model.

(left)   The large, abstract vases on the mantelpiece are made by frequent COLVILLE collaborator BRUTE CERAMICS.

Why fandoms are
now as influential
as the figures
they revere.

ESSAY:
FAN THE FLAMES

Words
TOM FABER

Picture a typical fan. What comes to mind? A Trekkie wearing pointy Spock ears at a sci-fi convention? A teenage girl screaming at a One Direction concert? Comic Book Guy from *The Simpsons*, guzzling slushies and haggling over a mint-condition *Batman* figurine? Or perhaps one avatar in a virtual horde, tearing across Twitter to wage war on a rival fan group?

You might note that none of these images cast fans in a positive light. Despite many formerly maligned fandoms going mainstream over the past decade—think of Marvel, expanding from geeky comic subculture into the biggest film franchise on the planet—such unkind stereotypes remain our automatic reference points. But the essence of fandom is innocent—it's feeling passionate about something and sharing that with a community. So how did it get such a bad rap?

as the word "fan" is an abbreviation of "fanatic" from the Latin *fanaticus*, meaning "of a temple" or "inspired by God." Just as religion seems inscrutable to many atheists, fandom is often a mystery to nonbelievers. "To people outside it's like, 'Why would you be so interested in that thing?'" says Hannah Ewens, author of the book *Fangirls: Scenes From Modern Music Culture*. "It makes people curious and suspicious. Why would you bother giving all your time, resources and love to this thing that doesn't know you exist?"

After speaking to hundreds of fans for her book, she realized the answer was multifaceted. "It's about fun, escapism, feeling understood," she says. "It's almost like falling in love; you can feel that obsession hook into you." A fan's relationship to their hero is described in psychology as "parasocial"—a dynamic where one person extends

> " It's almost like falling in love;
> you can feel that obsession
> hook into you."

According to Mark Duffett, professor of Media and Cultural Studies at the University of Chester, "Media fandom is the recognition of a positive, personal, relatively deep, emotional connection with a mediated element of popular culture." The phenomenon is not new—Hungarian composer Franz Liszt received such frenzied receptions at his performances in the mid-19th century that the phenomenon was dubbed Lisztomania. Admirers would clamor to seize his discarded handkerchiefs and broken piano strings. In the 20th century, significant fandoms formed around Elvis, The Beatles, and sci-fi franchises such as *Star Trek*, *Doctor Who* and *Star Wars*.[1] Outside of the arts, sports fandom invokes similarly intense tribalism, and occasional violence, among its devotees.

Commentators often reach for the language of religion when describing this love—we speak of "worship" and "idols." There is a precedent here,

intimacy and emotional investment while the other is unaware of their existence.[2] In some ways, this makes a fan's love safer than that of a romantic relationship. "The object of fandom isn't going to hurt you," says Ewens. "It's only going to give you positive feelings and be a mirror for how you're feeling about it."

The scope of fandom was dramatically broadened by the arrival of the internet, which enabled enthusiasts to find each other more easily and to join in creative pursuits such as fanfiction and fanart on platforms including LiveJournal, Tumblr and DeviantArt. Many make lifelong friends

(1)   After The Beatles' guitarist George Harrison mentioned he was partial to a British candy called Jelly Babies in a 1963 interview, fans soon began sending him packets in the mail and pelting him with them at concerts.

(2)   "To be a fan is to scream alone together..." Ewens writes in *Fangirls: Scenes From Modern Music Culture*. "It means pulling on threads of your own narrative and doing so with friends and strangers who feel like friends."

and receive vital emotional support from these groups. While this community aspect is important, most people emphasize that the central relationship is the individual one, between the fan and the object of their passion. "Being a part of the Lana community didn't directly change my life," says a user who goes by Marta, who co-runs the largest Lana Del Rey fan site, "but her music and her message did."

It used to be that artists had to rely on magazine interviews to communicate with fans, but today they can speak directly via social media. This makes the relationship feel more intimate; where once the stars of the silver screen were untouchable ciphers, today's idols are just a message away. Superfans have adopted collective names such as

" Whereas offline fan culture is contemplative and creative… online 'stan culture' is where things start to get toxic."

Taylor Swift's "Swifties," Beyoncé's "Beyhive," Justin Bieber's "Beliebers," Ariana Grande's "Arianators," and Lady Gaga's "Little Monsters."[3] These groups express appreciation through discussion, image sharing or coordinating campaigns to boost their idol's success. They might listen to new singles on repeat to drive them up the pop charts or mass-buy products the artist sponsors to help them secure more branding deals.[4]

However, the centralization of online fandom onto social networks also created the conditions for more volatile communities to emerge. "Whereas offline fan culture is contemplative and creative, fundamentally about warmth and community, online 'stan culture' is where things start to get toxic," says Ewens.

(3)   Lady Gaga famously nurtures her fanbase, and has even tattooed the words "Little Monsters" on the arm she uses to hold her microphone.
(4)   Last year, fans of BTS and Blackpink exerted their power in an entirely different realm: political activism. They took credit for helping to inflate expectations for the poorly attended Trump rally in Oklahoma by reserving tickets they had no plans to use.

The word "stan" is derived from a 2000 single by Eminem which narrates the story of Stan, a fictitious fan who writes to Eminem repeatedly and, frustrated by the rapper's lack of response, drives his car off a bridge with his pregnant girlfriend tied up in the trunk. A word first coined to describe an obsessive stalker was gradually claimed by certain groups on Twitter as a badge of belonging and pride.[5]

By representing fandom as a slippery slope to psychopathy, Eminem is drawing on a reductive stereotype, yet there is genuine cause for concern at the fringes of online fandom. Stan groups see themselves as online guardians of their idol's reputation. They wage virtual wars on detractors, using social media pile-ons, review bombing (flooding review sites with negative feedback) and doxxing (publishing someone's private information online). Ariana Grande fans chased her ex Pete Davidson off social media after their breakup. Lady Gaga fans inundated Ed Sheeran with messages, forcing him offline following a perceived slight. And a group of Michael Jackson fan clubs in France launched lawsuits against the two men who accused the star of sexual abuse in the 2019 documentary *Leaving Neverland*. Fortunately, both Gaga and Grande de-escalated the situation by posting online asking their fans to calm down.

Why do stans rally in defense of an artist who doesn't really need defending? "They're not fighting for the artist, they're fighting for themselves," explains Ewens. "They've aligned their identity so closely with this artist—they see themselves almost like an employee or a close friend. An attack on the artist feels like an attack on the fan." These frenzies have sparked a moral panic about toxic fandom in the media. Yet perhaps they are best understood not in the context of fandom, but in the context of social media. For decades, these communities have existed mostly peacefully in their own communities—first as real-world fan clubs, and then online on bespoke fansites. It has only been in the last five years, as the groups have migrated to social media and stan culture has emerged, that things have gotten ugly.

Unlike on fansites or forums, the organization of information on social media is not democratic. Social networks are designed according to an economic model that monetizes audience engagement and profits by selling data and advertising space. Therefore algorithms prioritize content that is engaged with most frequently—hot takes, loud voices and extreme opinions, for example. When coupled with the fact that social media users often fall into "echo chambers"—meaning they only see content representing one ideological viewpoint—it's clear that the architecture of social networks pushes online communities toward tribalism and extreme behavior, whether they're a group based around music, politics or sports.[6]

The fact that fandoms are labelled "toxic" while other volatile online communities fly under the radar is simply a symptom of how the media has demonized fan culture throughout history. "Fans have long been used as a barometer for social anxieties," Duffett explains. "In the 1960s, people were worried about promiscuity and latched onto the idea that fans were groupies. In the era of 1980s individualism, media commentators saw extreme fans as stalkers. Today society is concerned about trolling, loss of privacy, and the dark side of collective action. The media simply uses fandom as a way to speak about these things."

Fan groups are often subjected to demeaning stereotypes because the nature of the phenomenon is surprisingly tricky to pin down. It may seem simple to understand why someone is a Justin Bieber fan, but the inquiry rapidly spirals into unwieldy philosophical questions: Why do we like anything? Why do we feel things? Why do we want to belong to groups? Fan culture is inherently plural and polyvalent. People engage in fandom both individually and as part of vast, complex networks. They define themselves by drawing deeply from the outside world. They fall into wild love affairs that are exciting, nourishing and never need to be requited; these abiding relationships offer one thing that is sure in a world of churning uncertainty.

(5) One Eminem fan broke the world record last year for having the most portrait tattoos of a musician. She has 16 images of the rapper on her body.

(6) In the 2020 US presidential election campaign, many candidates' supporters began to identify as "stans." Political stanning, wrote *The New York Times* in 2019, "is a new way of seeing democracy, and of obscuring it."

Kevin ÆBSTRACT:

Words
SHARINE TAYLOR

THE ARTIST CONSIDERS HIS CULTURAL LEGACY.

Photography
EMMAN MONTALVAN

(previous)   Abstract wears a jacket and trousers by BILLY HILL.
(above)   He wears a vintage jacket by PATAGONIA, a vintage shirt, jeans by DREW HOUSE and shoes by FUGAZI.

Kevin Abstract wears many hats. A rapper, producer and songwriter, he first made a name for himself as one of the founding members of Brockhampton. For the Corpus Christi native, having flexibility and space to explore creative pursuits, both new and old, is a top priority, but he's also thinking through how everything he attaches himself to will become part of his cultural legacy. "I wonder what Brockhampton will be 10 years from now?" he says, speaking from Los Angeles. "What did we mean for the culture, to hip-hop and music? What was our role in all this?"

The last year afforded ample time for the *Arizona Baby* artist to slow down and think purposefully about the creative climate he's cultivating. "Hopefully that inspires anyone I'm working with to be performing at their best as well," he says.

SHARINE TAYLOR: Have you learned anything new about yourself during lockdown?

KEVIN ABSTRACT: I've learned that I want to try to get back to making things from a pure place. Being able to sit around and have the luxury to think has made me realize that a lot of the things I've been making for the past few years weren't coming from there. It was me creating things that made people like me more. That's where I'm at now: doing things because I love doing them.

ST: Sometimes, the way we think about time (or the lack of it) informs how we approach the things we love. What have you learned about the intersection of the two?

KA: There's no need to rush. If I could go back and tell myself anything, it would be to have more patience. I'm approaching every project now with focus and not rushing for success. A lot of the time I was doing stuff, I was just trying to get out of whatever situation I was in, financially or with family. It was me trying to find a way out. You can make things from that place—pain, or whatever it is you're dealing with—and still learn to be more patient.

ST: Do you embrace vulnerability in your music, or hold back?

KA: I try to put it in the music. There are things I'll say online, in an interview or in a song that I would never say to my friends and family. I've learned to use this medium as a way to express myself, but sometimes I don't know if that's coming from the purest place. Like I was saying earlier, it's from me trying to find a way out. Not as much now, but early on. I wouldn't dare tell my mom I was gay, but it was easier for me to do it online or in my music because I knew people would connect or it would help someone else in that situation. In order to really make it, I felt like I needed to be vulnerable. That was a tactic I was using to help myself deal with that pain.

ST: That sort of vulnerability transforms you. It's a form of reinvention, but an authentic one.

KA: Yeah, it can help you turn things you don't like about yourself into strengths. Then you become some sort of superhero and use those things as powers.

ST: How do you navigate the different perspectives between your birth identity, Clifford Simpson, and the performer Kevin Abstract in day-to-day life?

KA: I feel like you have to be mindful of it but I try to just do my best. Whatever it is I'm doing, whatever someone asks me to do, I try to do my best and give people the best thing. That's all I feel like I can do and control.

ST: Are you interested in exploring film?

KA: One thousand percent. I want to be able to do whatever I want, whenever I want to do it. That's kind of what I mean about making things from a pure place. I wanted to put a short on Brockhampton's YouTube channel. It'd be cool to do that and I can make it right now, but I want to be able to make

Styling
NICK HOLIDAY

(below)   Abstract wears a jacket by VIDEO STORE APPAREL, a vintage hoodie by RUSSELL ATHLETIC and holds a hat by HOLIDAY.

" In order to really make it, I felt like I needed to be VULNERABLE."

the best thing. That's what I mean by patience and taking time to get to the version of me that I aspire to be.

ST: Imposed artistic limitations can stop artists from pursuing different things.

KA: Every few months I'm inspired to do or build something new. I need to create a playground for myself where I can go and make the movie, make the album, produce the album or produce a video for someone else. [I always want to] have access to creating whenever I feel inspired or whenever I want to help inspire people to make things.

ST: What was the process behind creating the *Roadrunner: New Light, New Machine* album?

KA: A lot of studying, research and pushing myself and the guys to be at their absolute best. It was the most time

we've ever spent on a project which is cool because we came up making three albums in six months. To take time with the project has been very sobering—a bit of a wake-up call to say this is what we've missed out on this side of creating. The other approach also works, but it's cool to see other sides because there are so many different ways to make an album or a song.

ST: What's the biggest difference you noticed creating *Roadrunner* with what you've experienced before?

KA: It makes me wonder if we're better when we're being prolific in making things very fast. When I say better, [I mean] if people like us or will like us more when we spend a long time on one thing. Prince has so many albums

[that are] very prolific in a way and Michael Jackson's discography was way more focused.

ST: What do you want to be a vessel for?

KA: I want to empower people who feel like they have no one around them and give guidance or strength to [help them] make something out of their lives. I want to do my best to make the world a better place. It might sound a bit cheesy but it's exactly how I feel.

(above)
Abstract wears a sweatshirt by RAF SIMONS.

(left)   Abstract wears a sweatshirt by RAF SIMONS.
(below)   He wears a sweatshirt by RAF SIMONS, trousers by HOLIDAY and shoes by SALOMON.

(overleaf)   Abstract wears a jacket by RAF SIMONS, a vintage hoodie by EVERLAST, trousers by BILLY HILL and shoes by BETTER GIFT SHOP X SALOMON.

" I try to do MY BEST
and give people the best.
        That's all I can control. "

114	Earth 2.0
130	Do the Robot
138	The End Games
142	Sara Seager
150	Future Flags
156	Report: The Diigitals
160	Archive: Bodys Isek Kingelez
164	A Survey of the Future
168	Patent Pending

Part 3.
FUTURE
Forecasts from space, art and avatars.
114 — 176

A second turn
on the third rock
from the sun.

EARTH 2.0

Photography
MICHAEL
OLIVER LOVE
Styling
LOUW KOTZE

(left)   Yoyo wears a bodysuit by STYLIST'S OWN, stockings by WOLFORD, a balaclava by CRAIG PORT and shoes by THAT SHOE LADY.
(above)   Samuel wears a cape by KLÙK CGDT, stockings by WOLFORD, a bodysuit by STYLIST'S OWN and a balaclava by CRAIG PORT.

(above)   Yoyo wears a balaclava by CRAIG PORT.
(right)   Yoyo wears a top and cape dress by GAVIN RAJAH and a balaclava by CRAIG PORT.

(above)   Yoyo wears a dress by VIVIERS and a bodysuit by STYLIST'S OWN. Lebone wears shorts and a cape by VIVIERS,
             a bodysuit by STYLIST'S OWN and a balaclava by CRAIG PORT.
(right)   Yoyo wears a top and cape dress by GAVIN RAJAH, a bodysuit by STYLIST'S OWN, a balaclava by CRAIG PORT and shoes by THAT SHOE LADY.

(below) Samuel wears a dress by VIVIERS, a bodysuit by STYLIST'S OWN and a balaclava by CRAIG PORT.
(right) Yoyo wears a dress and cape by VIVIERS and shoes by THAT SHOE LADY.

Makeup
MICHELLE-LEE COLLINS
Models
LEBONE SEBOLAI &
YOYO BONYA at My Friend Ned
SAMUEL at Outlaws

DO THE ROBOT
A study of dancing androids.

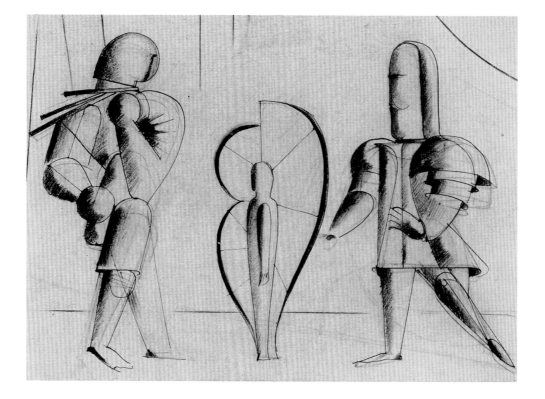

Words by
Stephanie d'Arc Taylor

Dance is associated with the emotional pinnacles of the human experience—love, joy, lust, art, insanity. Watching someone dance, or doing it ourselves, inspires emotions we struggle to access otherwise. This complicated relationship between movement and feeling is part of what makes us human. It makes sense, then, that artists and researchers working with robotics view the creation of a dancing robot as a meaningful tech frontier: How better to prove the skillful yet fundamentally unthreatening potential of humanoids than getting them to do the Mashed Potato?

The engineering company Boston Dynamics released a video in 2020 that went viral for its skillful robot choreography. One figure has a head, two legs and two arms. Its physiology mimics our own, so watching it dance like we do (or maybe more like our grandparents did) doesn't look unnatural. But when other robots get on the floor, things get weird. There is a hybrid dog-snake robot that performs a delicate *bourrée en couru*—the series of tiny steps a ballet dancer takes on almost straight legs. Another kangaroo-shaped contraption appears to be able to twerk. The strange implications of dancing robots reach far beyond their meticulously programmed chips. Here, we approach its cultural significance from five distinct viewpoints.

I.

ROBOT COSTUMES

The project of the Bauhaus, the legendary 20th-century interbellum German design school, was to create a *Gesamtkunstwerk*—a comprehensive artwork—in which many disciplines are brought together. But Bauhaus artists didn't just concern themselves with typical art forms like painting, sculpture, dance and typography. Rather, reflecting the preoccupations of the age, Bauhaus luminaries devoted themselves to understanding—and forging—relationships between art and technology to serve humanity.

Oskar Schlemmer was hired by the Bauhaus in 1923 as a master of form—meaning he was mostly in charge of theater productions. The costumes he designed for dancers performing in his pieces were outsized and colorful, with well-defined shapes; he described them as a "party of form and color." The geometry of the costumes juxtaposed with the fluid form of the human body in motion was meant to build connections between the seemingly disparate forms. Humans and machines, the costumes seem to tell the viewer, don't have to exist in separate vacuums.

Schlemmer's hopeful vision of this happy marriage might seem antiquated today, as concerns about encroaching artificial intelligence are raised with each passing news cycle. But we can take heart when reviewing Schlemmer's costumes: Technology also offers whimsy and joy.

II.

ROBOT TEACHER

There may not be many people who wish to learn partner dancing without having to touch another human being. But thanks to a research team at Tohoku University, this hitherto underserved group of would-be waltzers now has their dreams fulfilled: There is a robot that will teach you to waltz.

It looks as unsettling as it sounds. The robot's base is made up of three wheels that start off leading the dance and then adjust to the partner's movements. The wheels are connected to a cylindrical torso of sorts, above which is a "head" consisting of a screen that displays real-time feedback to the waltzing human. Rounding out the robot are two "hands," one of which the student is meant to grasp as the other reaches around in a metallic embrace, to rest on the student's shoulder blade.

Dancing, insofar as it involves physical pleasure, is a sensual art form. Even when partner dancing doesn't involve physical touch, there is an inherent intimacy in the experience of shared movement. An empathy gap is a factor when considering the future relationships between humans and robots. Robot-human dancing may be remembered by our great-grandchildren as the first step toward shared experience.

III.

ROBOT CHOREOGRAPHY

Catie Cuan has worked with almost every commercially available robot in her career—both choreographing for them and dancing with them. She's now in the process of completing a Ph.D. in Mechanical Engineering at Stanford University. On her plate are questions as broad as the meaning of dance—and whether it can exist when divorced from the human form.

SDT: Are humans the only beings that can truly dance?

CC: Dance is something that exists in the universe—it doesn't need a human body. My new piece is inspired by the motion of birds and bees and anything that swarms. To make a swarm is an incredibly simple algorithmic task. The rules are: first, detect bodies around you, second, maintain the same distance, and third, maintain the same orientation. You can give those rules to triangles on a screen, or to 20 robots, and you have a swarm. That's dance.

SDT: What is the appeal of dancing with a robot instead of a human?

CC: I love humans—I want to make choreography for humans all day long, but I feel a transcendence when I'm dancing with a robot. I feel a collapsing of time; it's a process that's physically and spiritually compelling. It's different from the intellectualizing I do all the time about robots.

IV.

THE ROBOT

If you were in mime school in the 20th century, you would probably have learned the Mannequin Dance: a jerky yet rhythmic series of movements meant to mimic the presumed movements of a humanoid form. The word "robot" came into use in 1921, and as the world became fascinated with automation over the next decades, the dance took on a new name. By the time the mime Robert Shields performed the dance for television heavyweights Merv Griffin and Johnny Carson in the 1970s, the dance was known as the Robot.

Today, the dance is canon, familiar to even the most dogmatic pop culture refuseniks. That's not because of Robert Shields, though. The Jackson 5 began performing the Robot to their smash hit "Dancing Machine" in 1973—and the youngest brother, Michael, took it from there. The Robot became one of his signature moves. Even his Moonwalk has similar robotic elements of popping and locking.

In terms of movement, Michael Jackson may have been the 20th century's most influential person. His dance moves will certainly be emulated by future generations—which means in our lifetimes we may actually have the pleasure of seeing an actual robot doing the Robot.

V.

ROBOT SKEPTICS

The choreographer Michael Kliën, who is now the director of the dance program at Duke University, was one of the first in the dance world to explore the possibilities of working with computer software and artificial intelligence, in the late 1990s and early 2000s. He's also skeptical that AI and dance have a future together.

SDT: Why are people so fascinated with making robots dance?

MK: Well, "choreography" means to write dance. I tell people what to do and they do it in a particular way and that's choreography. Of course, this ideology can easily translate into robotics because you can tell robots what to do and where and when. But this is not an interrogation of what makes us dance in the first place.

SDT: So why do we dance?

MK: Frequently we dismiss the ideology that forms the dance in the first place. Different cultures have different dances, they access the dancing state for different reasons: political and social reasons, rites of passage, spiritual reasons, or all of those together. In societies, dance is a kind of language.

SDT: Robots can't dance, then?

MK: Robots don't dance. Robots present the programmer's vision of dance.

"I love humans... but I feel a transcendence when I'm dancing with a robot."

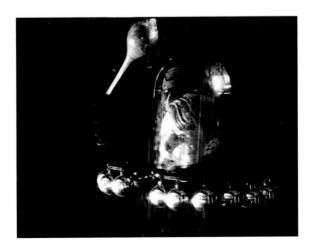

(below)   Photograph: T. Lux Feininger © The Estate of T. Lux Feininger. Repro: Art-Archives.net (Catalogue Raisonné)
(right)   Photograph: Fine Art Images/Heritage Images/Getty Images

FUTURE

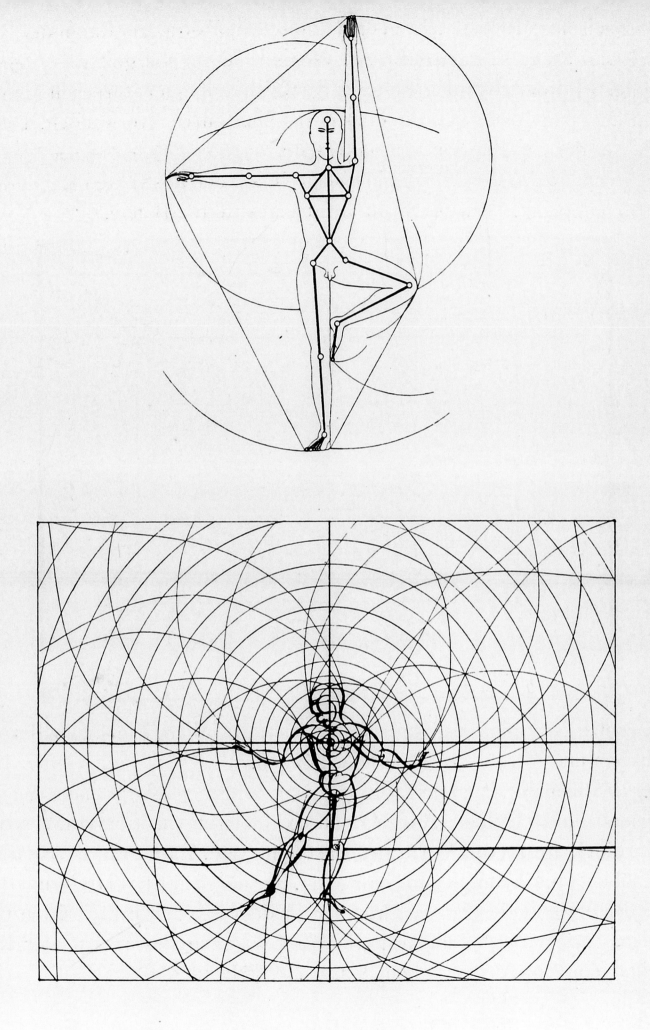

A cultural primer
for the end of days.

ESSAY:
THE END GAMES

Words
HETTIE O'BRIEN

The phrase "unprecedented times" has become an axiom for the present, but it's less an accurate description than a banal truism. After all, a condition of thinking about the future is that we assume our own moment stands in extraordinary relation to it, and that we must be living through the end. But we might never know when the end has really arrived.

Last year, the number of people preoccupied with the end of the world grew from a core group of religious fundamentalists and conspiracists to include just about everyone, as the fast clip of 24-hour news announced the terrifying consequences of COVID-19. A poll of American citizens conducted in the first months of the pandemic found that 29% of adults think there will be an apocalyptic disaster in their lifetime.[1] This could be a sudden event—an asteroid, a nuclear war—or an

underwent a profound shift during the Enlightenment, when people started to think about the end of the world in terms of human extinction rather than judgment day. "The central insight of the Enlightenment is the idea that values are something that are made by humans," he tells me.

When we are dead, those values die with us. Nothing is harder to imagine than nothing, which is why a supernatural apocalypse is intuitively easier to grasp than a secular extinction event that wipes out humanity, such as a deadly pandemic or an astrophysical disaster. Apocalypse is a leveler where everyone will be judged equally in the eyes of God (and even rich fossil-fuel executives will meet with fiery wrath). Annihilation, on the other hand, is a void—the absence of everything we know.

Where apocalypse offers the sense of an ending, the losses we now face—in the shape

" People have been worrying about the end of the world since the beginning. It is always on the horizon, never having arrived."

accumulation of incremental catastrophes, the climate crisis being the most obvious among them.

And yet, despite everything, it was still possible—if you worked from home—to switch off: to play video games, cook dinner and ignore the news. This is what makes the idea of doomsday so difficult to grasp. People have been worrying about the end of the world since the beginning: The idea is everywhere and nowhere at once, always on the horizon, never having arrived. Thomas Moynihan, an intellectual historian and author of *X-Risk: How Humanity Discovered Its Own Extinction*, believes our idea of the end times

of extinction and environmental breakdown—are better understood as "the ending of sense," Moynihan says. In the 20th century, after two world wars and the creation of the atomic bomb, fears about the end times came to be motivated less by biblical superstitions and more by a pragmatic anxiety that humans might actually be the authors of their own ends. Moynihan refers to these human-made disasters as "doomsday" scenarios, a term which gained currency during the Cold War, when it was used to refer to the potential fallout from nuclear weapons.[2]

The clearest (and most gimmicky) encapsulation of this fear is the Doomsday Clock, which resembles a quiz-show timepiece and is supposed to indicate the spiraling threats to humanity in the form of things like artificial intelligence, nuclear war, climate change and pandemics. It's set every year by the Bulletin of Atomic Scientists, an

(1)   The survey also found that men are considerably more likely than women to back their survival odds: 49% of men thought they would survive a week or more, compared to 36% of women.
(2)   The threat posed by nuclear weapons goes far beyond the explosion itself. Scientists have modelled how the resulting smoke would block out the sun for an extended period, plunging the world into a deep freeze.

organization founded in 1945—immediately after the bombings of Nagasaki and Hiroshima—by scientists who had been involved in the Manhattan Project. The hands of the clock are always set before midnight, signaling the point of human catastrophe, but how many minutes and seconds before midnight depends on how optimistic the scientists are feeling. In 1991, after the end of the Cold War, the clock was set at 17 minutes to midnight. Currently, we have 100 seconds left before the end starts.[3]

But for whom is the world really ending? Those who seem most concerned by these eventualities—the smooth-faced Silicon Valley billionaires buying up New Zealand, doomsday preppers and James Murdoch (the youngest son of Rupert

"No amount of canned beans will allow you to escape the reality that everyone around you is dead."

Murdoch, who is rumored to have built an "apocalyptic" bunker in Canada)—tend not to find themselves at the sharp end of the last days.[4] Theorizing about the end of the world "can seem like [a] pastime for white, male, rich middle-class professors, whereas the world has already ended for lots of people across history," Moynihan says. Taking doomsday seriously is an indulgent mental exercise that presupposes humans would have a reasonable idea of how it will actually play out. That's why planning for the end times can seem hysterical; no amount of canned beans will allow you to escape the reality that everyone around you is dead.

(3)   In a statement to the press, Bulletin justified its 2021 calculation by pointing out that "the pandemic revealed just how unprepared and unwilling countries and the international system are to handle global emergencies properly."

(4)   Several US billionaires fled to their New Zealand bunkers in March 2020. However, according to manufacturer Rising S Co, at least one had to call up to ask for the door code.

Popular culture has tried to address such fears. In a 1965 essay about science fiction films, the American essayist Susan Sontag described the "lure of generalized disaster" inherent to such movies, which allow a release "from normal obligations" and give an outlet for "cruel or at least amoral feelings." Films about the end of the world tend to either be set during a sudden and cataclysmic event, as with the freeze of *The Day After Tomorrow*, or after the event itself has occurred. And in *The Last of Us*, a video game first released in 2013, the player traverses a post-apocalyptic version of America, fighting off zombies in a survivalist fantasy.[5] But we rarely see the end of the world as it will likely occur: an incremental descent into a worse version of now.

There are a few exceptions. *Children of Men*, Alfonso Cuarón's 2006 film, has been widely praised for its dystopia, a deathly amplification of the present.[6] And I'd wager that the lesser-known *Years and Years*, the HBO drama set in Britain during the 2020s, is similarly effective. The program follows an extended family into the next decade, as they navigate the perdition of Britain's hostile environmental policy, a rapidly decaying biosphere and the consequences of automation. The series works because these events simply provide the background to the show's narrative: Its focus remains on the family members and their relationships with one another.

Although bad things do happen (a nuclear explosion takes place, an authoritarian politician is elected prime minister, the glaciers have already melted), life goes on, and the family is still forced to endure its attendant banalities. When their father dies, knocked down by a "Rideroo" bike at the age of 69, it's not the collision that kills him but a scratch on his hand that develops into sepsis. "They tried all the antibiotics, but they don't work anymore," says his son.

Will we even want to think about the end of the world after the pandemic is over? If those who spend the most time worrying about an apocalyptic event are, paradoxically, the furthest removed from its consequences, then those closest to disaster tend to find enjoyment in other forms. During the First World War, the French painter Claude Monet devoted his time to his panoramic oil paintings of the water lilies in his garden at Giverny. From his house, he could hear the gunfire in the distance and would see wounded soldiers trudge down the road. "I'm a bit ashamed," Monet wrote near the end of the war, "thinking about little researches into form and color while so many people suffer and die for us."

Amid the dry invective of social media and the briefings of dazed politicians pronouncing daily death statistics, it would hardly be surprising if people didn't want to think about the apocalypse anymore. Right now, aren't form and color, beauty and escapism, what we'd all rather be thinking about? In other words: If you need me, I'll be looking at the water lilies.

(5)   Research by the Stanford scholar Angela Becerra Vidergar has demonstrated that interest in survivalist fiction tends to rise in the years after a crisis like World War Two, rather than during.
(6)   *Children of Men*, released in 2006, is set in 2027 and imagines a world beset with natural disasters and widespread infertility.

Sara SEAGER:

Words
ROBERT ITO

ON THE HUNT FOR ANOTHER WORLD.

Photography
VALERIE CHIANG

Sara Seager, an astrophysicist and planetary scientist at MIT, has been searching for worlds beyond our own solar system for decades. Dubbed exoplanets, these heavenly bodies had been something of a mystery within the scientific community, right up until the time Swiss astronomers discovered one of them, the enormous 51 Pegasi b, in 1995. Exoplanets are among the most exciting finds in astronomy—many would argue they're *the* most exciting—because they offer the promise of life on other planets. Black holes and supernovas are swell in their own way, of course, but the long-held dream of astronomers, poets and sci-fi fans alike has been to find proof that we humans are not alone in the cosmos.

When Seager first began studying exoplanets, many wondered if they even existed. Because stars are so bright, they have the same effect as a spotlight in a room full of candles; if you take a photo of a planetary system, the only thing that gets processed is the light from the star. Those Swiss scientists hadn't actually seen 51 Pegasi b, only observed the gravitational effect it had on its sun-like star.[1] Among astronomers at the time, studying exoplanets was akin to looking for aliens. Even if they did exist, they were so far away, how would one begin to learn even the most rudimentary things about them?

Today, the once-niche field is booming. "Many of the best and brightest who enter this field are going into exoplanets," Seager says. "And the public loves them. It's like science fiction come true."

Much of that boom can be credited to Seager herself, who has become one of the field's most celebrated scientists, securing prestigious awards in astronomy and physics for her pioneering research into exoplanet atmospheres. She is also widely recognized for her TED talks, mentoring up-and-coming female scientists and appearing in publications from *National Geographic* to *The New York Times Magazine*. In 2013, she won the MacArthur Fellowship, aka the "genius grant," for "quickly advancing a subfield initially viewed with skepticism by the scientific community."

On a recent afternoon, Seager was in her home in Concord, Massachusetts, talking about how she came to find herself studying things that are absolutely enthralling and yet, in many ways, totally out of reach. Consider 51 Pegasi b. Decades after its discovery, scientists still haven't seen it, let alone any of the other thousands of exoplanets identified since. And you can forget about going there. At some 50 light years away from Earth, it would take nearly one million years to reach in a conventional spacecraft. Given those obstacles, it's tough to fathom how much we'll know about the planet and its ilk in the foreseeable future.[2] For astronomers like Seager, it's something to think about. How does one stay motivated when this year's research project might not bear fruit for years or even decades, if at all? "As all of us get older, sometimes you see your goals slip away," Seager says. "When I was a lot younger and just starting out, there were older people who were the

age I am now, or even older, and I saw them retire and not meet their goals, because the stars didn't align."

With such temporal concerns in mind, Seager is embarking on a new project, one much closer to home, relatively speaking. "My life goal has kind of changed," she says with a laugh. "I still want to find another Earth and signs of life on a planet far away, but that life goal might not be attainable. So I got involved with a new opportunity, and that's on the planet Venus." The surface of Venus (average temperature: 864 degrees Fahrenheit) is too hot to sustain life, despite what fantasy writers like Edgar Rice Burroughs and C.S. Lewis might have theorized about the planet and its weird inhabitants. But its clouds are not. Recent studies of the gases around Venus suggest that there might be life in the atmosphere—an organic gas living among the droplets.[3]

After years spent searching for signs of life in some of the most distant areas of the cosmos, Seager has taken up the hunt right here in our own galactic backyard. "Long story short," she says, "I'm now leading a mission concept study to send a probe directly to Venus."

(1) If an exoplanet doesn't orbit its star in a perfect circle, it will cause the star to move position slightly in a periodic way. One way of finding exoplanets is therefore by looking for wobbly stars.
(2) If there is life on another planet, it is likely to exist in what scientists call the "Goldilocks zone": a planet of a similar size to our earth, and a similar distance away from its star.

> " The public loves exoplanets.
> It's like science fiction come true."

Seager first felt the tug of the night sky when she was 10 years old. Unable to sleep during a camping trip with her family in Ontario, Seager snuck out of her tent and was staggered by the sight of thousands of stars on a clear, moonless night. It wasn't until years later, however, during a visit to the astronomy department at the University of Toronto, that Seager discovered that one could actually stare at stars for a living. "I was 16 years old, and I just couldn't believe how wonderful that was," she says. "That was one of the best days of my life."

In the ensuing years, Seager got her first telescope, fell in love (with Mike, her first husband, a freelance editor and lover of the outdoors), and went to graduate school at Harvard, where she found her fascination with stars and the night sky at odds with the "exercises in abstraction and tedium" that often come with the actual study of astrophysics. During her second year there, Seager considered quitting. The discovery of 51 Pegasi b helped change all that, inspiring Seager to move from studying the Big Bang and its aftermath—a worthy endeavor, but one that Seager struggled to find her place in—to exoplanets.

Seager wrote about her experiences —both personal and astronomical—in her inspiring and often heartbreaking memoir, *The Smallest Lights in the Universe*, which was published in 2020.[4] In the book, Seager describes how she lost Mike, the father of her two boys, after an agonizing bout with cancer, and how she struggled to cope with life after his passing.

" Saying you're an ASTROPHYSICIST can make people feel awkward...

She joined a support group of young women called the Widows of Concord, but even within this most welcoming of makeshift families, Seager hesitated to reveal what she did for a living. And who can blame her? There's no way to say "I'm an astrophysicist at MIT" without sounding like you're bragging about how smart you are. "It can make people feel awkward, and then it makes me feel awkward," she says. "And then people don't want to talk to me."

This is funny, because in person—or at least over our COVID-mandated Zoom call—Seager is the most open and engaging person one could hope to meet. Part of this is due to her absolutely disarming way of answering anything you throw at her with utter focus and sincerity, no matter how simple-minded or personal the question. *What's the coolest exoplanet?* That changes a lot, she tells me, like your "favorite book or film," but she currently has a thing for a class of planets called "mini Neptunes." *Do you believe in God?* She doesn't, in part because when she was nine or so she had a friend from India who had "her own personal goddess" among many while she, a Hebrew school student, had only one, and how could both stories be true? *When astronomers get together by themselves, what do they geek out over, besides telescopes?* Rockets, of course, and commercial space flight companies like SpaceX. *Have things gotten better for women in the sciences?* "I might have to say no."

She also has a charming way of making connections between her own experiences and yours, and of finding the human in what might otherwise be unfathomable. As we're chatting about our (separate) visits to the SpaceX rocket facility in Hawthorne, California—hers as an esteemed astrophysicist, mine as a nosy reporter who weaseled my way in as an excuse to see rockets—she wonders if I went to their coffee bar, or their ice cream bar, which are supposed to be pretty good (I did not). When she's talking

about the process of working on a particularly knotty problem in astrophysics, she asks if maybe I go through that same sort of thing too, say, when I'm trying to structure a story?

I ask if she and her colleagues ever think about life forms on other planets and what they might look like or be like, or if she ever thinks about going to those planets and living on them. Not so much, she says, except when friends or family or journalists invariably ask. She tells me about planets where the atmosphere is so massive that every day would be worse than the smoggiest day on Earth, or ones where the gravity is so immense that the animals there would have to have giant, elephant-like legs and really short bodies just to get around. Is this something she thinks about for work, I ask, or just for fun?

"It's for fun, mostly," she says.

In many ways, she's the perfect advocate for astronomy, able to make the often abstract and unimaginable come alive through the sheer force of her own enthusiasm. A glorious peek at the night sky set Seager on this journey of a lifetime, and you get the sense that it still thrills, albeit in different ways.

Sara Seager still has many things she'd like to do. There's the mission concept study to lead, to look for signs of life or perhaps even life itself, up among the Venusian clouds. She also hopes to spearhead the Starshade project, which involves creating a gigantic sunflower-shaped structure, 85 feet across, that would fly between a space telescope and a star, blocking out the star's light to reveal any surrounding exoplanets. She shows me a model of one, created at 1% scale, that she has on her shelf. Its steely points are sharp enough to draw blood, she tells me. This one was recently put through its paces in the dusty desert atmosphere of California's Death Valley. She often brings it along to talks she's giving, to get people

excited about the project. "It's for public outreach primarily," she says. "But since there's no public outreach now, I just keep it at home as a decoration."

Next to the Starshade model is a globe, but not just any globe. Instead of a tiny blue and green Earth, this globe is a model of the night sky with Aquarius and Ursa Major and Orion laid out across its inky surface. It was a gift from a man who had worked for the government his entire career, but hoped to go to graduate school to pursue a second career in astronomy. Despite the fact that he was a relative layperson, Seager directed him to one of her "planet finding" teams at MIT. He's now a member of the team, searching for planets during his free time.

"He was so grateful," she says. "So he sent me this gorgeous gift." She shows me its surface, and how the globe can spin in all directions. It really is beautiful, a miniature version of the glorious panorama that had so entranced Seager as a young girl. The man even had it personalized with a little plaque. Below her name, the inscription reads "Brilliant discoveries guided by those who inspire us to look within."

"I wasn't expecting this, because I see teaching and outreach as just part of my job," she says. "I was just so..." she begins, and then her voice trails off. "That's why I have it here," she continues. "Because it reminds me to be open to the universe, to give to the universe, and it will give back."

(3) Last year, a team of astronomers led by Jane Greaves of Cardiff University detected the presence of poisonous gas phosphine in the atmosphere, which they hypothesized could only have been produced by a living organism.

(4) In the book, Seager also writes about realizing she was autistic relatively late on in her life. "I'd been struck by something, a physical impact. So much of my life suddenly made sense," she writes.

and then it makes ME feel awkward. "

FUTURE FLAGS
Five flags that symbolize a future state of mind.

OPENNESS

Change happens so fast that even people of the same generation can feel estranged from those just a few years either side of them. Being open to new ideas is a critical precursor to unified action on global issues. It is also of personal benefit: study upon study shows

that being receptive to new ways of thinking is one of the key ways to stave off cognitive decline. For this flag, Pantoja drew on symbols of the open ocean and sky: a reminder of the vast geographical areas we have yet to fully understand.

Designs
JUAN PANTOJA

WONDER

During the COVID-19 pandemic, "awe walks" became a popular coping mechanism. The phrase describes a mindful practice of focusing one's attention outward while in nature and noticing the wildlife, weather and changing seasons. This quiet observation of the wonders around us is a good way of breaking from stressful thoughts, and an important resource for anyone hoping to experience the wonder of the world from right where you're standing. Pantoja designed this flag to look like the sun.

Photography
CECILIE JEGSEN

PATIENCE

The internet has made us nimble multitaskers, but it has deadened our ability to defer gratification. In a 2017 YouGov report, almost half of all respondents said that technology had made them more impatient than they were five years ago. There are some aspects of life

where speed is a virtue (commuter transport, for example, is better when efficient) but many more where good things come to those who wait. Pantoja's design for this flag is inspired by waves—which return again and again and symbolize calm, steadiness and reliability.

UNITY

In early 2020, it seemed like COVID would result in people sealing themselves off and living in isolation. But the communities that coped best with the pandemic were often the opposite: neighborhoods where everyone knew each other, and where resources could be safely pooled or help offered. Many planners are now reconceptualizing the design of towns and housing to facilitate this sort of interconnectedness, and the unity and resilience it fosters. Pantoja's design is again inspired by the sun—the ultimate shared resource.

EQUITY

Equality is the belief that all people should be treated equally. Equity goes further and asserts that sometimes people need different resources in order to have access to the same opportunities; one popular cartoon on the subject imagines it as three people of different heights being provided with boxes of different sizes in order to see over the same wall. Pantoja's flag is inspired by the branching leaves on a tree: they are all individual, but stem from the same fundamental source of life.

REPORT:
THE DIIGITALS

Meet the human running the first digital supermodel agency.

Words
ALLYSSIA ALLEYNE

Artwork: Courtesy of The Diigitals

There's a pattern to the way people profile a new female fashion model. First, there's the intro describing her exquisite, conventionally attractive looks. To follow, the writer homes in on a few distinctive characteristics that might humanize her—the scattering of moles, the gap between her teeth—before getting to the campaign, film or magazine where the reader is likely to have seen her. In several recent profiles, this generic intro is followed by the big reveal: The model isn't real at all. She's actually one of the many computer-generated models who have been slowly infiltrating the fashion industry over the last few years.

This is how many people learned about Shudu, branded across the web as "the world's first digital supermodel." Designed by Cameron-James Wilson, a British fashion photographer turned amateur digital artist, Shudu first went viral in 2017. Initially, viewers on Instagram—including

and *Cosmopolitan*. At the 2019 BAFTA awards, she walked the red carpet as a hologram.

In April 2018, Wilson turned his project into a business with the launch of The Diigitals, which he bills as the world's first all-digital modeling agency. Today, their roster has expanded to seven models, including Brenn, a plus-size model, and Galaxia, an alien with iridescent blue skin. The company offers bespoke models and generic presets that can be modified to fit clients' needs.

"I just thought it was a super cool idea. It sounded like something from *Black Mirror*," Wilson explains, speaking from his home in Weymouth, a coastal town in the south of England. "I believe in creating the future that you want to live in, and I want to live in a kind of *Blade Runner*-esque future."

A lot of people share his vision. Beyond Shudu, the world has been captivated by the likes of

> " I believe in creating the future that you want to live in, and I want to live in a kind of *Blade Runner*-esque future."

Naomi Campbell, Tyra Banks and Alicia Keys—shared, liked and marveled at her lean physique, elegant neck and radiant dark-brown skin, debating whether her beauty was too good to be true.[1] But it was only after Wilson outed himself as her creator in 2018, ending the speculation, that Shudu really caught the industry's attention. Soon after, Wilson was tapped by Balmain to create its first CGI campaign, starring Shudu and two other models dressed in the French fashion house's pre-fall 2018 collection. She has since gone on to model for Ferragamo, Samsung and Lexus and to be featured in editorial shoots for *Vogue Korea*, *WWD*

Imma, a diminutive influencer with a pink bob, who "designed" and modeled a limited-edition collection for Amazon; and Miquela Sousa, or Lil Miquela, who has a Calvin Klein campaign, a Prada collaboration, and three million Instagram followers under her belt.[2] Last year, both *Vogue Taiwan* and *Vogue Italia* featured bespoke CGI models on their covers, circumventing the challenges of arranging a photo shoot during a pandemic.

Others are less enthused, cautiously eyeing a near-future where real models will lose jobs to digital avatars who can look and behave however a brand desires, at what they assume will be a lower cost. For Wilson, who is white, the initial backlash was doubly loaded: Critics have accused him of trying to capitalize on efforts to diversify the fashion industry while taking jobs away from real, working Black models. (In a poorly received interview with *Harper's Bazaar*, he said Shudu was

(1)   Shudu was modeled on the Princess of South Africa Barbie doll. If Barbie's vital statistics were scaled to real life, she'd be forced to walk on all fours and would be physically incapable of lifting her own head.

(2)   An analysis by OnBuy, a British online marketplace, estimates that Lil Miquela makes around $10 million a year for Brud, the company that created her.

inspired by and represented "a big kind of movement with dark skin models.")

"All I wanted to do was make a beautiful image, and there was no money involved. I was literally creating these pieces of art," Wilson says in response to those early recriminations. Now that there is money on the table, Wilson says he tries to "include as many Black female creatives [as possible]" in Shudu's success. The Diigitals typically hires human "muses" to provide the poses and movements upon which he models Shudu, and he employs a Black writer, Ama Badu, to author Shudu's written voice.[3]

This isn't the first time that models' livelihoods have been threatened by perceived interlopers. Similar pearl-clutching took place in 1999, when The New York Times reported that American fashion magazines were shifting focus from "the placid, youthful beauty of models to the expertly pancaked visages of movie stars and talk-show hostesses," and again in 2016, when Vogue pondered whether social media would "ruin" modeling by giving an unfair advantage to amateurs with less talent, but larger followings.

" We're just scratching the surface of what the capabilities are. "

This isn't even the first time virtual models have been cast as the opposition: In 1999, when Elite Model introduced Webbie Tookay as the face of Illusion 2K—its short-lived and largely forgotten division for virtual models—the voluptuous blonde was positioned as a reliable alternative to the real supermodels Elite represented. As an agency spokesperson told the press at the time, here was a model who would never "complain about working long hours, never gain weight, never have to worry about boyfriends, lawyers or personal managers." (Elite co-founder John Casablancas, who spearheaded the launch of Illusion 2K, famously loathed the flesh-and-blood supermodels he profited from, including Naomi Campbell, Cindy Crawford and Linda Evangelista, who he denounced as "spoilt troublemakers.")

However, the idea that The Diigitals will make models obsolete feels overstated—not least because Wilson himself isn't buying into the hype. "I don't know if that's what the consumer wants," he says. "I think 3D models will become popular and have their users, but... the consumer obviously likes seeing real people—people who they know are real."

Influencer agent Jennifer Powell, who has been representing Wilson and The Diigitals since 2018, suggests it's limiting to only look at CGI models in relation to their human counterparts. "The opportunity isn't just in consumer-facing campaigns," she says. "We're just scratching the surface of what the capabilities are, not just in terms of digital influencers, but also B2B capabilities when it comes to brands designing in 3D, and helping in those workflow and design processes, and brands' sustainability narratives."

According to Wilson, 60% of The Diigitals' work is designing virtual fit models for fashion brands to use internally when designing prototypes on 3D imaging software—a strategy that is increasingly being adopted to cut down on waste during sample production. "I know a lot of people think that there's this kind of agenda to push out real models... No, a lot of companies just want it for boring internal visualizations and stuff like that," Wilson says. "You have these 3D mannequins for making the garments, but they just don't look that great in terms of realism."

In his view, the coronavirus pandemic has "fast-tracked adoption of 3D within the industry," with restrictions on travel and gathering forcing brands to find alternatives to traditional photo shoots and runway shows. And, this summer, The Diigitals will be expanding into e-commerce with a top-secret, high-profile collaboration at a time when lockdown orders have sent online spending to all-time highs. "In a lot of cases, it's more expensive, and it's a lot slower [than a photo shoot]," he says. "But you're being innovative... and you can do things and visualize things in a way that you couldn't before," Wilson explains.

Powell, whose human clients include fashion blogger Bryanboy and Sincerely Jules, has found that, when it comes to CGI campaigns, brands are more interested in "trialing new ideas and working with different artists and in different ways," than in replacing humans outright.

In fact, brands are already making room for human models in the digital world.[4] Last year, a CGI version of Kendall Jenner starred in a Burberry campaign video produced by Nick Knight. Natalia Vodianova, Irina Shayk and Imaan Hammam have all licensed their digital likeness to Drest, a virtual styling game.

"It's just a different story that you're telling," says Powell. "It's like the Marvel Cinematic Universe. Are those things real? No. But does the storytelling capture our imagination? Yes. And I think that CGI models have done the same thing."

(3)   On The Diigitals' website, Badu is listed as a muse. She writes that she wants "others to read Shudu's story and make a personal connection they hadn't realised they needed."

(4)   Humans are also making room for digital designs. In 2019, a digital dress sold for $9,500 to a blockchain security expert who bought it for his wife.

ARCHIVE:
Bodys Isek Kingelez

Words by
Aindrea Emelife

I invite you to ask yourself: If you could model your own utopia, what would it look like? If you could be the architect of a society, what would you include, exclude, multiply and decrease? Could you envision a political and social transformation?

Congolese artist Bodys Isek Kingelez took on this task with his beguiling and painstakingly intricate architectural sculptures, which he called "extreme maquettes." He made hundreds of these metropolises from found materials, exercising society's problems in cardboard and waste plastic and positing his view for the ideal society.

Born in 1948 in what was then the Belgian Congo—in an age of huge political and social transformation—Kingelez was 12 when his country gained its independence from the oppressive colonial regime. At 22, he relocated to Kinshasa—the capital of the newly independent nation of Zaire (now Congo). After university, he worked as a secondary school teacher for a short time.

Before long, Kingelez had an itch to scratch. He became, in his own words, "obsessed with the idea of getting my hands on some scissors, a Gillette razor, and some glue and paper." He started creating sculptures and forming his own architectural landscapes from modest materials such as paper, repurposed commercial packaging and cardboard. His sculptures were handmade dreams for his country at the moment of independence from Belgium, as well as for the African continent and the world at large.

Kingelez's eye for detail was further honed during a brief stint working as a restorer for the National Museums Institute of Zaire. The story goes that when he first presented the maquettes to the museum they thought the pieces were so sophisticated that they must have been stolen, and asked him to create another one in front of them. Kingelez acquiesced, and made *Commissariat Atomique*. Mouths hit the floor. The museum offered him the position of a restorer, a role he held for six years, but Kingelez ultimately committed to fashioning his utopias full time.

At the same time, President Joseph Mobutu was building with great speed. His futuristic buildings signaled a departure from the art deco style of the country's colonial past. Still, these projects were only accessible to the very wealthy. Kingelez's work is both a reflection of civic pride in this new nation and a critique of Mobutu's despotism and perpetuation of inequality in the capital. In the catalog for MoMA's *Bodys Isek Kingelez: City Dreams*—Kingelez's first US retrospective—Chika Okeke-Agulu, a Nigerian art historian, writes that it is a "spectacular architectural form as a counter-narrative to the dystopian realities of Kinshasa."

The worlds Kingelez created would have been an optimistic departure from his day-to-day experiences of urban life. He made no preparatory drawings, instead formulating his work in interaction with the material. But Kingelez was not the "naive" artist he has sometimes been portrayed as. With a university education and an international outlook, he was a visionary polyglot with a great sense of industrial design. Kinshasha was growing rapidly due to urban planning, and Kingelez understood the ramifications of this growth on economic inequities. He also believed that architecture had the power to affect the way people live and work.

Kingelez's dream cities are spectacles to behold. Art deco accents soar into the sky. Spayed, fan-like structures peacock among the architecture. Skyscrapers are counterpointed by colorful, wavy apartment buildings in juicy oranges and yellows. Slick office complexes zig and zag to the heavens. It is intentionally bright, bold and dizzying, small but beautiful, stupendous yet orderly. There is optimism in his color choices. Even his *Scientific Center of Hospitalisation the SIDA* (1991), created at the peak of Congo's AIDS crisis, is given a powder pink and zesty

" The worlds Kingelez created would have been an OPTIMISTIC DEPARTURE from his day-to-day experiences of urban life."

blue treatment with colorful stars. Kingelez himself had a penchant for impeccable and flamboyant dressing, much like the Congolese sartorialists known as *sapeurs* whose crisp, bright three-piece suits served as a revolt against the social, political and economic difficulties of post-colonial society.

Kingelez set out to solve the world's ills.[1] One piece, the eight-foot-wide *Ville Fantôme* (1996), envisions a city with no police force or military. The work is just as urgent today, when the Defund the Police movement seeks to reallocate funds to non-policing forms of public safety, rehabilitation and community support. Kingelez also looked to Palestine, creating his *Centrale Palestinienne* in 1994. A honeycombed structure that supports another glittering tower, rendered in the colors of the Palestinian flag, it was created after the first Oslo Accord confirmed Palestine's right to self-govern. That same year, he celebrated the 50th anniversary of the United Nations with a stand-alone structure decorated with stars to represent the equality of the countries, and a flashing "UN" sign at its spire.

Kingelez, who died in 2015, worked at the same time as popular Congolese painters Chéri Samba and Moké, both of whom also reflected on contemporary life. He was a private person, however, and sat on the sidelines of the art world until his major debut in the 1989 exhibition *Magiciens de la Terre* in Paris. The exhibition was the focus of some controversy: While expanding the

Eurocentric canon of art, it also reinforced the "otherness" of art from the "non-West."

Magiciens de la Terre attracted the interests of mega-collector Jean Pigozzi. Despite this, and the support of influential Nigerian curator Okwui Enwezor—who championed the work through his scholarship—Kingelez's work is still largely an enigma, with little academic focus on his oeuvre, either in his home country or abroad. Remarkably, Kingelez's triumphant 2018 exhibition was the first monographic show dedicated to a Black African artist in MoMA's history. Sarah Suzuki, the exhibitions curator, says she was intrigued by his vision: "That incredible combination of compositional sophistication, technical adroitness, and wild invention and the pure visual joy that he created in each one of his sculptures."

Although Kingelez's utopias are rendered on a tiny scale, the changes they imagine are vast—not just individual buildings, but cities, countries and the world. His art is a reminder that dreaming catalyzes doing.

(1) In an artist's statement, Kingelez wrote of his belief that art had the power to transform and help build a better global society: "Art is the grandest adventure of them all... art is a high form of knowledge, a vehicle for individual renewal that contributes to a better collective future."

A

Five future-focused thinkers on what comes next.

1.
(HOW WILL WE COMMUNICATE?)

of

2.
(WHAT WILL WE WEAR?)

5.
(HOW WILL WE TRAVEL?)

6.
(WHAT WILL SEEM LIKE A DISTANT MEMORY?)

Survey

3.
(WHAT WILL HOMES LOOK LIKE?)

4.
(WHAT WILL WE EAT?)

Interviews
GABRIELE DELLISANTI

7.
(WHAT CHALLENGES WILL WE BE FACING?)

8.
(WHO WILL BE POWERFUL?)

Future.

What might the world look like in 50 years?

As 2020 demonstrated, our ability to look even a year beyond the present moment is limited. Expand that timeline to half a century, and the shape of the world is anybody's guess. For the Future Issue, we eschewed a single oracle and instead asked for the predictions of five people in very different industries: a sci-fi writer, a neuroscientist, two futurists and a cyborg anthropologist. Their answers, which oscillate between saccharine utopianism and cynical pessimism, are a telling reminder of just how little we can foresee. The survey also reveals an interesting dichotomy in how we think about the future: Is it better to predict the future we actually think will come to pass, or the one we wish to see?

— HOW WILL WE COMMUNICATE?
AC: The medium by which we communicate may change, but what we communicate will stay the same: music, art, film, worship, love.

EC: I don't think our way of communicating will get better or worse. It'll just go faster. And it'll be more and more dependent on tech companies.

KA: What might come to mind is the type of tech. But I think of linguistics—things like memes and poetry, short fragments of text, images, video or sound that are layered with meaning because of how they are shared, and which are shared so fast.

DE: The future will drift away from cellphones in favor of more direct ways of communication. We will broadcast by making subtle movements of our muscles and understand inputs through patterns of vibration on the skin. This will allow us to always keep our eyes and ears open for other stimuli in the world.

AO: More slowly—with a realization that all of the speed we've become accustomed to has caused a lot of unsustainable practices in our lives.

— WHAT WILL WE WEAR?
AC: We'll be wearing things that are made for the long-term again, looking back at the 2020s as the throwaway area. We'll want to learn again, maybe understanding how meaningful it is to make hand-dyed linen with local berries.

EC: Just nostalgia. People will look back and see what they think is cool and bring it back. We'll keep having that 20-year nostalgia loop. Now we're looking back at the '90s, and so on.

KA: From a tech point of view, we'll see layers of embedded sensing in the clothes we wear, things that might charge electronics or measure data around us.

DE: I think we will have active clothing that isn't just for fashion and warmth but for communication and sensing.

AO: The same things we love, just for longer. The pandemic laid bare the facade of needing newness. Throwaway culture doesn't really add that much joy to our lives.

— WHAT WILL HOMES LOOK LIKE?
AC: They're going to be much more tuned to the environment. Like, a desert home will look different from one in the Pacific Northwest. I think homes are going to be cozy, and there will be a deeper understanding of natural light because of a greater push to conserve energy.

EC: That depends on the class of the person. I could see the rich having smart homes, the middle class living in discount smart homes and the poor just having to live in the same rundown apartments they've been in for the last 200 years.

KA: There's this option that allows for the coming together of more kinds of families in one home: adapting to working, living and being with a bubble of people.

DE: In my book *Livewired*, I've proposed that homes will eventually be able to utilize the principles of plasticity that we see in biology.[1] So if you are using the kitchen more, it will grow in size. If you have guests, and many people need to use the bathroom, the number of toilets and sink spigots will grow to accommodate.

AO: Multidimensional spaces and multigenerational homes. People will reconnect with the joy of rootedness that balances home, work and play, and they'll welcome a much more diverse perspective on what co-living means—a co-living that spans generations.

— WHAT WILL WE EAT?
AC: Everyone will be eating bugs and thinking of cow meat as the most disgusting thing. We're also going to eat our trash because it'll be biodegradable. And, importantly, what we eat will be totally dependent on our local environment and match the climate.

EC: Same crap we always eat. I sound like a pessimist. But food is an economic thing. And unless the economy changes, healthy food won't be available to all people.

KA: Definitely fewer animals, more plants. And we'll have to eat even more plants because the nutrients of plants will be lower because of climate change. Lab-grown meat will be common too.

DE: All animal-based products, from meat to milk, will be replaced by lab-grown alternatives.

AO: Much of what we eat now. But with less of a focus on hyper-convenience, and more interconnectedness. This will mean only eating certain things at certain times, and eating what your community cultivates.

— HOW WILL WE TRAVEL?
AC: I see travel becoming more meaningful and longer-term. Right now, the entire world seems identical with the same chain stores and that isn't very fulfilling. We will be traveling for memory, discovery and preservation, and staying in places for longer, maybe

AMBER CASE
is an American cyborg anthropologist and futurologist specializing in the interaction between humans and technology. She's the author of four books and is based in Portland, Oregon.

ELWIN COTMAN
is a sci-fi writer specializing in urban and dark fantasy fiction. His latest work, *Dance on Saturday*, was published in 2020. Cotman lives in Oakland, California.

KRISTIN ALFORD
is a futurist and the director of MOD, a museum of discovery at the University of South Australia, which showcases exhibits that seek to inspire people about the future and how to navigate it. She's based in Adelaide, Australia.

DAVID EAGLEMAN
is an American neuroscientist and author. His bestselling book of short stories, *SUM*, was adapted into a chamber opera. Eagleman is also the director of the Center for Science and Law, an independent nonprofit which works to bridge the gap between neuroscience and law.

ANGELA OGUNTALA
was born in New Jersey and works as a director at Greyspace, a Copenhagen design and foresight consultancy which works with different organizations to provide ideas about what a desirable future might look like.

spending six months in a small Japanese village to learn centuries-old crafts.

EC: I could see automated travel becoming big. It's one of those things that looks weird until it becomes ubiquitous. See it this way: An airplane ride is 90% automated. So if we've normalized that, then we can normalize travel in robot cars.

KA: There will be a desire for less energy-intensive transport. For air travel, I'm thinking about this scenario where in 2042 the last leisure air flight will have landed and from then on it's just freight.

DE: By launching passenger-filled rockets straight up into the air and then having them fall as the Earth rotates. In this way, we will be able to reach distant destinations much more quickly than we can now.

AO: When we travel, we'll stay in places for longer, and have fewer quick jaunts. This is also tied to the understanding that we will have to become accustomed to finding more comfort and excitement in our nearer surroundings.

— WHAT FAMILIAR THING WILL
SEEM LIKE A DISTANT MEMORY?
AC: Plastic. The idea of throwing stuff away after you use it will be so laughable. Like, you're on a plane and you throw away five items every time you eat? Ridiculous. Also, people who don't know how to cook. Are you kidding? The idea of living in a small container and having everything sent to you will seem backward and wrong.

EC: Patience. I worked with high schoolers born into social media and they just live in that high-velocity world. And it's not like they're social media junkies, it's just the world they live in.

KA: The thing that comes to mind is the pencil. I still use a heap of pencils for work. And it's just one of those things that seem so enduring but will disappear.

DE: Judgments—good or bad—based on skin pigment.

AO: Routine business travel. People will be much more discerning about when they actually need to travel long distances or get on a plane for work. We've seen too much of what's possible remotely when it comes to the practicalities of work.[2]

— WHAT CHALLENGES WILL
WE BE FACING?
AC: We will still have to fix and learn how to live alongside nature.

"Things will break. People will break things that are unfair."

EC: Obviously, climate change and the mass extinction that comes along with it. It's real, it's happening and nobody in any government has yet made a considerable effort to do anything about it. Humans should be coming together to fight global warming, but I don't see that happening.

KA: Social inequities. And if we're serious about shifting gender or racial inequity, people who now hold the current power will be giving up things, and that's hard.

DE: With AI's takeover of most jobs, the challenge will be how billions of humans will fill their time.

AO: Figuring out how to make sense of the world we see around us, especially as things like shared values and understandings feel like they are slipping away. We'll need a lot of support and collective sense-making to understand what "good" looks like and how to act in a period of mass transitions.

— WHO WILL BE POWERFUL?
AC: The people who share the most. Anything. Whether it's ancient rituals or a better process for farming. And nature... nature will be powerful.

EC: Putin. Look at the US—we have the greatest military in the world, but almost no power. The power is in the hands of people who control the money, who have the thought power.

KA: Change comes from the outsiders challenging those who hold power. Today power is held by wealthy, white, Western men. But I see young women shaking the cage. And it'll be through collapse—sorry, but that's how systems change. Look at Russia, Hong Kong. Things will break. People will break things that are unfair.

DE: The programmers.

AO: I think storytellers will be powerful. As we feel inundated with all the noise and friction and uncertainty around us, those who can tell a story to make sense of the world, to bring us comfort and belonging will be powerful.

(1) In *Livewired*, Eagleman calls machinery that can reconfigure itself "liveware." He proposes that this livewired machinery will function in much the same way the human brain is able to absorb and adapt to new environments.
(2) Efforts to contain the COVID-19 pandemic saw air traffic plummet. For the week starting January 4, 2021, the number of scheduled flights worldwide was down by 43.5% compared to the week of January 6, 2020.

New additions to
the cosmos of useless
contraptions.

PATENT PENDING

Photography
LUC BRAQUET
Set Design
CHRISTIAN
FELTHAM

(previous) WIRELESS SEABUDS: Enjoy the ambient sounds of the ocean through these wireless conch shell earpieces, then return them to the waves as sea levels rise around you. Sanjay wears a jacket by AMI and a shirt by MAISON KITSUNÉ.

(above & right) FANCY FLOOR SHOES: Your digital footprint may be stamped all over the virtual world, but you can leave no trace behind in the real one thanks to these stylish sponge-soled dress shoes. Sanjay wears trousers by HOMME PLISSÉ ISSEY MIYAKE.

CHINDŌGU

These designs were created in collaboration with set designer Christian Feltham and were inspired by the Japanese craze *chindōgu*—the art of creating a product whose usefulness is precluded by its absurdity. The term was coined by Kenji Kawakami, a former editor at a Japanese mail-order magazine. Kawakami was strongly opposed to materialism and capitalism, and created inventions that were ill-suited to mass production as a rebuke to mass-consumerism. However, one generation's useless invention can be another's day-to-day reality: Kawakami's 1995 book *101 Un-Useless Japanese Inventions* included an early protoype for the selfie stick.

—

Styling
GEMMA BEDINI
Grooming
ALEXIANE GUYON
Model
SANJAY APAVOU

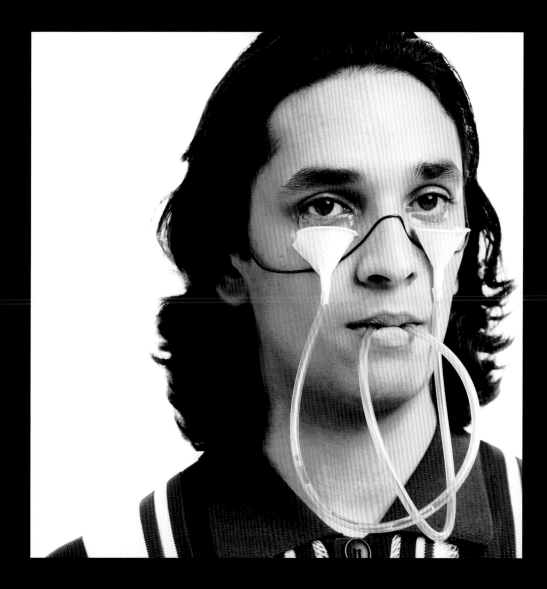

(left)   HOLIDAY-AT-HOME SLIDES: Don't take your flip-flops to the beach, bring the beach to your flip-flops! Help reduce air travel with this new holiday shoe design that really puts the "sand" back in sandals. Sanjay wears trousers by NAMACHEKO.

(above)   HUMAN HYDROPONIC SYSTEM: Water will be a scarce resource in the future. While you lament the decline of civilization, this tear harvester will funnel any emotional run-off into a handy personal hydration system. Sanjay wears a shirt by LANVIN.

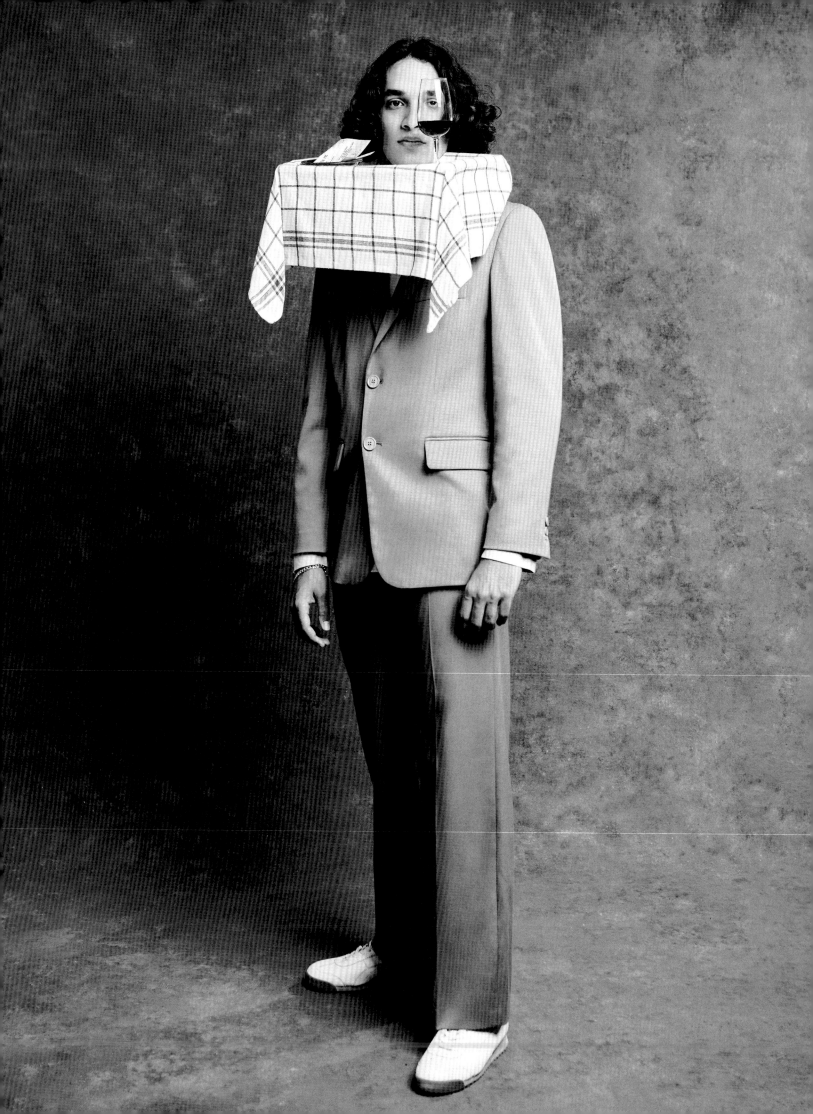

(left)   TABLE FOR ONE: Stuck at the office, but wishing you weren't? Just add your own legs to this portable tabletop to experience the pleasure of dining out again. Sanjay wears a jacket and trousers MM6, a shirt by HOMME PLISSÉ ISSEY MIYAKE, sneakers by MAISON KITSUNÉ X PUMA and a bracelet by VIBE HARSLØF.

(below)   THE CRUMB CHUM: Get out of crummy situations with this handy clip-on fan. Simply attach it to a lapel or collar and watch as it effortlessly blows away the delicious but dastardly debris from croissants and so much more. Sanjay wears a shirt by LOUIS VUITTON.

(overleaf)   ALL-IN-ONE GROOMER: This outsized personal grooming device will allow you to keep one step ahead of lockdown hair during future global pandemics. Thanks to a full-head combing capability, neat and tidy hair now can be acheived in one fell swoop. Sanjay wears a shirt by AMI.

178   Peer Review
179   Object Matters
180   Cult Rooms
182   Beverly Glenn-Copeland
184   Bad Idea
185   Good Idea
186   Crossword
187   Correction
189   Last Night
190   Credits
191   Stockists
192   My Favorite Thing

Part 4.
DIRECTORY
Addendums, archives
and a puzzle.
178 — 192

Words:
Zoë Blade

Composer ZOË BLADE on the pioneering, otherworldly and sometimes uncomfortable music of synth maestro WENDY CARLOS.

I first heard of Wendy Carlos more as a legend than an artist. I was too young to witness firsthand the impact of *Switched-on Bach*, the album that formally introduced synthesizers to the world. I came to her music through her later collaborations with Stanley Kubrick on *A Clockwork Orange* and *The Shining*.[1] The two working together seems somehow inevitable: Both were perfectionists, poring over every detail.

Carlos was born in Rhode Island in 1939. Her musical education began at the age of six, practicing on a drawing of a keyboard, and ended with a master's degree in composing electronic music at Columbia University. In the 1960s, she provided important feedback on the first commercial synthesizers to be developed, pushing Bob Moog to revise and refine his devices. She convinced the world that this odd new instrument wasn't just worth paying attention to, but that it was the future.

Always a pioneer, Carlos worked from her home studio when such a thing was unheard of, most people having neither the money to afford such a setup, nor the mastery of electronics required to maintain it. Her apartment on Manhattan's Upper West Side in the 1960s and '70s boasted a cozy nook crammed with tapes, knobs and wires, the technology offset with potted plants for a homier feel. By the '80s, she'd moved down to Lower Broadway, replacing much of the aging analogue equipment with modern digital counterparts. It's easy now to romanticize Carlos' original setup, not in spite of, but because of its limitations. As an electronic musician, I'm inevitably influenced by her, although it is her workflow rather than her style that has had the greatest impact: building music up one note at a time, crafting each sound from scratch. In a world with countless distractions, I've found this kind of approach to be an oasis.

As for Carlos, her music remains unparalleled. She elevates once-familiar classical pieces into haunting, otherworldly forms, both quaint and futuristic. Even now that synthesizers have become commonplace, her technique remains singular. The world may have caught up with her technology, but no one has yet matched her craft.

(1) I would recommend *A Clockwork Orange: Wendy Carlos's Complete Original Score*. Carlos' renderings of classical pieces featured in the film will likely be familiar even to the classical novice: *The Thieving Magpie*, *Beethoven's Ninth* and *The William Tell Overture* all make an appearance. Still, it's her original compositions that best showcase her musical abilities. To my mind, nothing does this quite so well as the album's opener, the epic "Timesteps." Although it was intended to gently introduce the vocoder—the device which lets synthesizers sing—I find it surprisingly grandiose, even frightening, in a way that's compelling. The album embraces how uniquely scary synthesizers can be, in the right hands. Carlos does for waveforms and filters what Kubrick did for light and shadows.

OBJECT MATTERS

Words:
Stevie Mackenzie-Smith

A searching history of the crossword.

As pastimes go, crossword puzzles enjoy a pretty virtuous reputation. Why scroll grids on Instagram when you can tackle a real one with a freshly sharpened pencil?

Like so many new forms of entertainment, however, when the crossword debuted it was regarded with suspicion. First published in 1913, the "Word-Cross Puzzle" was the invention of Arthur Wynne, a British expat editor at Joseph Pulitzer's broadsheet

New York World. His was more literal than cryptic. "What this puzzle is," one of Wynne's first clues read: "HARD."

Today, *The New York Times* publishes a hallowed crossword puzzle, which starts easy-ish on Monday and culminates in a brain-tangling crescendo on Sunday.

Ironically, the newspaper of record was initially sneering, calling the crossword "a primitive sort of mental exercise." The paper's writer thought idle wordplay was sinful—likely to corrupt American minds. But the public adored it. Wynne and his colleague Margaret Petherbridge struggled to keep up with enthused postal submissions.

A change of mind at *The New York Times* came after the attack on Pearl Harbor with a nudge from the now-married Margaret Petherbridge Farrar. Writing to the *Times'* publisher, she argued of the puzzle's necessity in "an increasingly worried world." In words that ring true today, she added: "You can't think of your troubles while solving a crossword." She would become the paper's first crossword puzzle editor, fine-tuning Wynne's creation into the modern puzzle devoured over breakfast tables today.

Of course, having a broad fan base is not the same as having a broad approach to language. Historically, crossword constructors and editors have not employed language that represents the variety of America's lexicon.[1] A knowledge of opera, Latin and great white men would stand you in good stead. But today the tide is changing and younger constructors are making the crossword not just a fun pastime, but a richly fascinating survey of shared cultural knowledge. The crossword has always encouraged us to stay open and awake to unfamiliar possibilities. So next time you're faced with a grid, ask yourself: What new worlds might I learn about today?

(1) One practical reason for the general conservatism of crossword setters is that it is not a lucrative industry. Many crossword setters are therefore lifelong fans of the genre who turn professional only in retirement.

CULT ROOMS

Words:
Ana Kinsella

The Parisian apartment where
SAUL STEINBERG married fine
art with bathroom humor.

Photograph: Robert DOISNEAU/GAMMA RAPHO. © The Saul Steinberg Foundation/VISDA

Is there a better place to pass time at home than the bathroom? Shutting the door can feel like escaping into a world of the interior self.

For the Romanian-born American artist Saul Steinberg, the bathroom was not just a sanctuary—it was fair game. In 1955, the tiles of a Parisian bathroom provided a blank canvas for his playful drawings and explorations of the self at play and at rest.

Steinberg, born in 1914, was best known for his internationally exhibited art, and in particular his drawings for *The New Yorker* which spanned nearly six decades.[1] Whether on the cover of a magazine or the tiles of a French *salle de bain*, his graphic style is instantly recognizable. Characterized by the bold definition of his line, Steinberg's style gave shape to the witty ideas and observations contained in every work. In the postwar period, this made him something of an outlier—neither cartoonist nor fine artist.

While photos of the Steinberg bathroom float around the internet, the facts surrounding it are not as readily accessible. But Sheila Schwartz, research and archives director of The Saul Steinberg Foundation, is able to shed some light on its creation. In the early summer of 1955, Schwartz says, while staying in an apartment at 26 rue Jacob, Steinberg took to the bathroom walls with his paintbrush. This photograph was taken by the photojournalist Robert Doisneau, who took several shots both with and without Steinberg himself for a feature in *Vogue Paris*. Doisneau, known for his intimate and revealing images of life on Parisian streets, wasn't the only esteemed photographer to pay Steinberg a visit—his colleague Henri Cartier-Bresson also stopped by, documenting Steinberg's progress with the bathroom mural.

Schwartz notes that drawing on walls and furniture, "a kind of proto-installation art," had been part of Steinberg's artistic lexicon since the late 1940s. His 1949 compilation, *The Art of Living*, featured a series of drawings of women bathing. In a letter to his friend, the architect and writer Aldo Buzzi, he described the subject as "a whole unexplored and very decorative world with its tiles, ornamental fretwork, women bathers with little portions of their bodies sticking out of the water and so on."

Steinberg left Paris later on in the summer of 1955, and nobody knows exactly what happened to the bathroom after his time there was up. "Either the owner of the apartment washed off the 'decorations' after he left or they just faded away," Schwartz says. "The apartment was also probably renovated at some later point." Today, a trip down rue Jacob on Google Street View shows an upmarket, well-heeled neighborhood just a stone's throw from the Pont des Arts.

Tastes change, though today the artistic merit in Steinberg's drawings is obvious—beyond his own esteemed reputation, line drawings of female figures have gained a particular currency in contemporary interior design, and even the most elegant of homes may have a funny print or portrait hanging on a bathroom wall.

In his letter to Buzzi, Steinberg explained that he was "trying especially to do humorous things" with his work. With his refined take on bathroom humor, he was certainly ahead of the game.

(1) Steinberg created 85 covers for *The New Yorker*. His most famous, *View of the World from 9th Avenue*, showed the city in the foreground and the rest of the world drawn in sketchy detail behind it. Opinion is divided as to whether it is a celebration of New York as the center of the world, or a comment on the myopia of its inhabitants.

BEVERLY GLENN-COPELAND

Words: Sala Elise Patterson

Half a century on from his debut, the KEYBOARD FANTASIES composer is the next big thing.

Forty-five years. That's how long the Canadian-American musician Beverly Glenn-Copeland spent *not* waiting for fame. Book-ending that period are his debut album, released in 1970, and the 2015 rediscovery of *Keyboard Fantasies*, a record first released on a few hundred cassettes in 1986. In the intervening years, Glenn-Copeland, who goes by Glenn, worked at everything from delivering pizzas to composing for *Sesame Street* and appearing as a regular on the Canadian children's TV show *Mr. Dressup*.

The one constant was making music in serene obscurity, a process he describes as translating into song the audible transmissions sent to him from the "Universal Broadcasting System." In the last few years his ethereal music has resurfaced, and his albums *Keyboard Fantasies* and *Transmissions: The Music of Beverly Glenn-Copeland* reissued. He has performed at MoMA in New York and been the subject of a documentary film that covers both his creative journey and his transition to living publicly as a man. But, at 76, he says it is less about the glory than about the joy of being around to witness it.

SEP: I know your father played classical piano at home when you were little. What were some other early musical influences?

BGC: As a child I was listening to the piano repertoire coming out of Europe —18th and 19th centuries. But by the time I was 12, my father was playing jazz records. I heard a lot of Black big-band music. Later, I was listening to music from around the world—Chinese, Indian, West African drumming.

SEP: In the 1970s, you were on the cusp of "making it." But not long after, the prospect of commercial success waned. What was that like?

BGC: I went to Los Angeles in my late 20s and had a famous manager, Billy James. He thought he could get me a good record deal. But I didn't fit into any musical category, so it couldn't happen. When I realized that I just said, "I'm not going to worry about it. There's no point in spending time with it." So, I just continued writing the music that I was hearing.

SEP: What led to your comeback in 2015?

BGC: A gentleman in Japan was introduced to *Keyboard Fantasies*. He wrote asking for some cassettes to sell. I didn't know where they were at first because they'd been tucked away for 30 years. Well, he sold them in a few days and asked for more. Then he sold those in a week. Then a company in California asked for some—and sold theirs. In about three months, there were several record companies asking if they could put out the album.

SEP: You describe your music more as a philosophy to be shared with humanity than as a sound. It's interesting that for years you worked without lamenting the fact that you couldn't share it with more people.

BGC: I attribute that to my Buddhist practice, which I started when I was 29. I was raised Quaker and when I went looking for a spiritual practice [as an adult], I concluded that I needed something out of the East. Most practices, especially in Buddhism, are silent. But I found one where I could make sounds—Nam Myoho Renge Kyo. It suited me perfectly, and it had the same philosophical underpinnings as Quakerism.

SEP: *Keyboard Fantasies* was made with an Atari computer and a drum machine. Has technology been useful for you?

BGC: The computer allowed me to create orchestral sounds when I heard them but when nobody was there to join me in making them. I was also hearing sounds that could only be made by a computer, like the stars speaking. When this computer came out, I was able to write in a larger scope, things that no acoustic instrument could possibly duplicate.

SEP: Did you feel that you had to contort your musical style when you were composing for children's television?

BGC: No. I wrote for the shows the way I wrote for myself. But I tried to make things that kids could relate to. The way in which I felt shackled was not musically, but by who I was on the show.

SEP: Because you were living as woman?

BGC: Yes. Because at the time I was living as a female and, once I understood that I was transgender I was well aware that there was no way I could make that announcement. There was no conversation at the time about people who were on the spectrum. You were either heterosexual or weird; straight or going to hell.

SEP: You once predicted that you'd be famous after death. What's it like now that it's happened in your lifetime?

BGC: I'm grateful because I can actually be here to witness the effect of these pieces on people, which is what they were sent to me for in the first place. So, I'm very happy about that. I'm thrilled.

BAD IDEA: SMELL-O-VISION

Words:
John Ovans

The quixotic history of an improbable, impossible machine.

The movie industry is currently searching for ways to get butts back in seats. One thing it is unlikely to consider is resurrecting Smell-o-Vision, a much-hyped "immersive experience" that was meant to be the next big thing, then wasn't.

First introduced during the 1939 New York World's Fair by Hans Laube—a Swiss advertising exec-turned-"world-famous osmologist," according to the press materials—the premise was that theaters could be

rigged up with a system known as the "smell brain," which would release odors via tubing to individual audience seats.

The smell brain made its cinematic debut much later with the 1960 film *Scent of Mystery* starring Elizabeth Taylor, where aromas were central to the storyline. The smells emitted—which included pipe tobacco, shoe polish and perfume—mingled together in peculiar and unholy combinations. As *The New York Times* reported, "Patrons sit there sniffing and snuffling like a lot of bird dogs trying hard to catch the scent." Smell-o-Vision's grand premiere was also its farewell performance. The film was quietly retitled *Holiday in Spain* and redistributed without the smell track.

Laube's is just one of many valiant efforts to harness smell's evocative associations to take audiences deeper into a fictional world. One of the earliest attempts recorded is a 1906 screening of the Pasadena Rose Bowl Game at a theater in Forest City, Pennsylvania, where cotton balls were dipped in rose essence and suspended in front of fans. In this century, the seemingly boundless potential of digital technology has brought the idea back into circulation. The app-controlled Cyrano Scent Machine, a device you could plug into your smartphone to emit smells along with video, was touted as the next big thing in smart technology. Attempts to buy it today lead you to a 404 page.

The quest to create a smell-along experience that actually works will certainly be resurrected by some future dreamer with new tools to hand. For now, there are always scratch-and-sniff cards—most famously employed in 1981 by the transgressive filmmaker John Waters in *Polyester* as a parody of Smell-o-Vision.[1] Later on a DVD commentary track, Waters remarked that, "I actually got the audience to pay to smell shit!"

(1) On entering the theater, viewers were given "Odorama" cards. Instructions on the screen indicated when to sniff the scents, which included flatulence, model building glue, gasoline and smelly shoes. Waters later accused Nickelodeon of lifting his idea wholesale for the more family-friendly film *Rugrats Go Wild*.

GOOD IDEA: THE SMELL OF HISTORY

Words:
Harriet Fitch Little

Despite the faulty execution of Smell-o-Vision, there is no questioning the wider fact that smells have the capacity to transport us. This is why a team of researchers at various European institutions recently embarked on a $3 million project to identify and recreate the continent's lost smells. Called Odeuropa, the endeavor will deploy artificial intelligence to screen old texts for descriptions of smells as far back as the 12th century, as well as scanning period paintings for aromatic information.

History, the researchers argue, has sometimes been shaped by smell: Will Tullett, a smell historian at Anglia Ruskin University, gives the example of London's Great Stink—a hot spell in the summer of 1858 that finally convinced parliament to approve the construction of a modern sewage system, rather than dumping it straight into the river that flowed past the building's windows.

Even when smell isn't instrumental, it's often instructive. At the Rijksmuseum in Amsterdam, for example, the smell of horses, gunpowder, sweat and Napoleon's heady cologne (he carried a bottle in his boot) are offered on scent sticks to tour groups looking at Jan Willem Pieneman's 1824 painting *The Battle of Waterloo*. Odeuropa hopes to extend the use of smell within museums, taking us far further back in time than cinema ever could.

NEW DEVICES

Crossword: Mark Halpin

ACROSS

1. Swerve out of control
5. Uses Novocaine
10. Mars, Venus, etc.
14. It's carried by some performers
15. Egg producer
16. Make "A V" more like "AV," perhaps
17. Syria, in Biblical times
18. Got going
19. Pop star
20. New device producing a wail (but rather a bland one)?
23. Lyrical lamentations
24. Narnia's king
26. Film that takes place inside a computer
27. Hannukah coins
30. L.A. to Chicago dir.
31. Yvonne of *The Munsters*
34. Nipper's co.
35. NPR's Ira, acting as spokesperson for a new pest-control device?
40. Butter, sometimes
41. "You understand what I'm sayin'?"
42. A "si" asea
43. 2007 Peace Prize recipient
44. Put behind bars
47. Soak oneself
49. Utter quickly
52. New deep-thinking device (compact model)?
56. *Game of Thrones* heroine
57. Something that may be passed on

58. Cheering
59. Show surprise
60. Approximately
61. Exertion
62. Makes a selection
63. The Four Seasons, e.g.
64. Muddle in the middle?

DOWN
1. Part of a barrel or song
2. *On the Road* journalist Charles
3. More ridiculous
4. Achilles, Percy Jackson, et al.
5. Virtuous
6. One place to find irises
7. Epiphany figures
8. Maidenform merchandise
9. Bring into alignment
10. The Joad family, among others
11. "Danger! Danger!"
12. Buds' bond
13. Kate McKinnon's show, in brief
21. They may be queued or cued
22. Templeton, for one

25. Close by
27. Carp
28. Otherwise
29. *The West Wing*'s Rob
32. Film set largely in the Land of the Dead
33. Not at all close by
35. Seize
36. Outmaneuver an opponent, maybe
37. Violet hue
38. PC character set
39. "Most peculiar..."
43. Come together
45. The Canadiens' Jacques Plante, for one
46. Onegin or O'Neill
48. Quite a lot
49. Cake serving
50. Potpourri part
51. Challenges
53. Calamine lotion target
54. Hanson or The Dixie Chicks
55. Like some apples
56. Prior to now

CORRECTION

Words:
Katie Calautti

On the scary shortcomings of "fearless" philosophies.

Fighting fear is a lucrative industry. The US personal development market is projected to be worth over $13 billion by 2022, and niche organizations focusing on fearless living and courage coaching have cropped up within it. "Master fear," these gurus advise. "Re-wire your fear-based habits!"

But is the mastery of fear a worthwhile goal? Fear is a survival mechanism—a protection against the threat of physical violence, but also an internal GPS guiding us away from people and things that don't serve us and reminding us to live life to its fullest.[1] So a healthy dose of fear can actually do a world of good.

On a base level, fear reminds us that we're alive, and confronting it creates resilience. When we experience a threat, it's followed by the euphoria of release when the danger passes. This is, in part, why some people love scary movies—they serve up the terror-relief cycle in a controlled environment. In fact, processing fear in a group setting has been shown to create bonds between people. Some studies reveal that short-term stress responses in small doses can boost our immune systems and increase mental performance.

Fear is a tough but fair teacher, drawing a big red circle around emotions or scenarios we've been avoiding that may be holding us back. In this way, it's more of a guiding light than a grease fire to snuff out. If we're afraid to confront that bullying boss or pushy friend, then it probably means we're supposed to: Fear can manifest as tension in a toxic work environment or as stress in an unhealthy relationship, acting as intuition on steroids. It can also be a powerful motivator—fear of

illness reminds us to take care of ourselves, fear of losing a loved one helps us appreciate and communicate with them.

Perhaps it'd be more apropos to be less "fearless," and instead live with an awareness of fear without giving in to its control.

(1) Actual fearlessness might reasonably be regarded as a brain disorder. In 2010, the journal *Current Biology* reported on a woman who, as a child, had experienced damage to her amygdala—a collection of cells near the base of the brain. Throughout her adult life, she had never experienced fear—even when she was held up by a man with a knife. "She tends to approach the very things she should be avoiding," a representative of the study told *Wired* at the time.

Photograph: E. E. McCollum

LAST NIGHT

Words:
Bella Gladman

Photograph: Michael Avedon

What did digital strategist JIAJIA FEI do with her evening?

Having previously led digital teams at institutions including New York's Guggenheim and the Jewish Museum, JiaJia Fei launched her own company last year, strategizing for museums, galleries and artists. Naturally, Fei's approach to pandemic living is also a master class in strategic leisure.

BELLA GLADMAN: What did you get up to last night?

JIAJIA FEI : Last night was not unlike any other evening lately. Every day, on the dot at 6 p.m., I work out virtually with my trainer. I've had an unexpected fitness transformation. Having never exercised, suddenly I can do 50 to 60 push-ups.

BG: And for relaxation?

JF: My daily bath, where I listen to the podcasts I would have listened to on my commute, like *The Daily* from *The New York Times*. After, I cook dinner. I hadn't previously been motivated to plan my meals—living in New York, it's really easy to avoid it. But now that I'm focusing on nutrition and fitness, I love a tofu and vegetable stir-fry. Because I'm Chinese, it has to be accompanied by rice.

BG: How does this compare to life before the pandemic?

JF: I'd be at back-to-back events, from New York Fashion Week to dinners for art openings. Now, I don't have the fear of missing out! I'm secretly an introvert, performing as an extrovert. When things open up again, I'll only go to events that add value to my life, like dinner with friends, then dancing.

BG: Do you subscribe to the "no screens before bed" rule?

JF: I've tried, but it's difficult when you live in close proximity to screens. My solution is stepping outside. Biking in the city is my way to meditate—it's the only time I'm not looking at a screen. At the end of the day, I'll ride to the waterfront at Brooklyn Bridge Park.

BG: What's your bedtime routine?

JF: I do a face mask, and then switch on my Muji aroma diffuser—my favorite scent is called Happy. I've been collecting scents to zhuzh up my environment.

CREDITS

FUTURE COVER:	PHOTOGRAPHER STYLIST MAKEUP MODELS	Michael Oliver Love with Hero Creative Louw Kotze Michelle-Lee Collins with Hero Creative Lebone Sebolai and Yoyo Bonya at My Friend Ned Yoyo and Lebone wear bodysuits by STYLIST'S OWN, stockings by WOLFORD, balaclavas by CRAIG PORT and shoes by THAT SHOE LADY.
10TH ANNIVERSARY COVER:	PHOTOGRAPHER STYLIST HAIR MAKEUP MODEL	Zhonglin Chen Yu Weic Lin Fiona Li Chen Hsu Chen wears a bodysuit, boots and a fishnet paper dress by JISOO JANG.
FAN BINGBING:	EXECUTIVE PRODUCER PRODUCER	Wei Liu Mac Zhou
FRACTURED FREQUENCIES:	PHOTO ASSISTANTS	Yuanling Wang Yinghan Wang Sherry Liu
EARTH 2.0:	PHOTO ASSISTANT STYLING ASSISTANT MAKEUP ASSISTANT LOCATION	John Marks Thabisile Msibi Clanelle Burger Afrikaanse Taalmonument
SPECIAL THANKS:		Glenda A. Hazard Flemming Jegsen Helle Jegsen Didrik Wei Liu Neil Roberts

STOCKISTS:
A — Z

A	AMI	amiparis.com
B	BETTER GIFT SHOP	bettergiftshop.com
	BILLY HILL	billy-hill.com
	BOTTEGA VENETA	bottegaveneta.com
C	COLVILLE	colvilleofficial.com
	CRAIG PORT	craigport.co.za
D	DREW HOUSE	thehouseofdrew.com
E	ERDOS	erdos.cn
	EVERLAST	everlast.com
F	FUGAZI	fugazi.la
G	GAVIN RAJAH	gavinrajah.com
	GRETA BOLDINI	gretaboldini.com
H	HOLIDAY	holidaybrand.co
	HUNTER BOOTS	hunterboots.com
I	ISSEY MIYAKE	isseymiyake.com
J	JISOO JANG	@jis00jang
	JW ANDERSON	jwanderson.com
K	KENZO	kenzo.com
	KLÛK CGDT	klukcgdt.com
L	LANVIN	lanvin.com
	LARA KLAWIKOWSKI	laraklawikowski.com
	LOUIS VUITTON	louisvuitton.com
M	MAISON KITSUNÉ	maisonkitsune.com
	MAISON SANS TITRE	maisonsanstitre.com
	MIU MIU	miumiu.com
	MONCLER	moncler.com
N	NAMACHEKO	namacheko.com
P	PATAGONIA	patagonia.com
	PUMA	puma.com
R	RAF SIMONS	rafsimons.com
	RICOSTRU	ricostru.com
	RUSSELL ATHLETIC	russellathletic.com
S	SALOMON	salomon.com
	STYLIST'S OWN	@stylistsown_
T	THAT SHOE LADY	thatshoelady.co.za
	THOM BROWNE	thombrowne.com
V	VIBE HARSLØF	vibeharsloef.com
	VIDEO STORE APPAREL	video-store-apparel.myshopify.com
	VIVIERS	viviersstudio.com
W	WOLFORD	wolfordshop.net

MY FAVORITE THING

Words:
George Upton

LUCINDA CHAMBERS, interviewed on page 90, shares the story of her mother's ring.

The first thing I notice about people is their hands, and whether they are gardeners or craftspeople. I think it resonates with me because I love working with my hands, even if I'm just doing papier-mâché or making a lampshade. It was something my mother instilled in me. I suppose styling is really just an extension of that.

Growing up we were a very crafty family. My mother did bookbinding and marbling, and my brother was a wonderful ceramicist. We would go to Harrods, measure the clothes and make them ourselves at home. When I left school, my mother and I went to art school together—in those days they gave you a grant that you didn't have to pay back. My mother did amazingly well; I did unbelievably badly.

She wore this ring every day of her life that I knew her, and now I wear it every day, still sewing, still making things. It's a signet ring, but her crest, a unicorn, and her motto *Pactum Serva*, "keep your word" have been carved into carnelian rather than gold. It's very battered and there's a chip missing from where my first boyfriend caught her hand in a car door. He was mortified but I think the ring saved her finger.

Photograph: Alex Wolfe